George Dawson

Pleasures of Angling with Rod and Reel

For Trout and Salmon

George Dawson

Pleasures of Angling with Rod and Reel
For Trout and Salmon

ISBN/EAN: 9783337144708

Printed in Europe, USA, Canada, Australia, Japan

Cover: Foto ©Andreas Hilbeck / pixelio.de

More available books at **www.hansebooks.com**

"MY FIRST SALMON." Page 66

PLEASURES OF ANGLING

WITH

ROD AND REEL

FOR

TROUT AND SALMON.

BY GEORGE DAWSON.

He that hopes to be a good Angler must not only bring an inquiring, searching, observing wit, but he must bring a large measure of hope and patience, and a love and propensity to the art itself; but having once got and practised it, then doubt not but that Angling will be so pleasant that it will prove to be, like Virtue, a reward to itself. — WALTON.

NEW YORK:
SHELDON & COMPANY.
8 MURRAY STREET.
1876.

PREFACE.

Most of the sketches which make up this volume were published in the *Albany Evening Journal*, at long intervals, during the past three years. Their title indicates their character and purpose, namely, to set forth the "Pleasures of Angling" by detailing some of the incidents common to its pursuit. If they shall afford any pleasure to the "simple wise men" who enjoy the innocent pastime and the quiet repose which no other recreation affords in such full measure, I will not regret that they have been given a form which was not originally intended.

G. D.

No life, my honest scholar, no life so happy and so pleasant as the life of a well-governed angler; for when the lawyer is swallowed up with business, and the statesman is preventing or contriving plots, then we sit on cowslip banks, hear the birds sing, and possess ourselves in as much quietness as these silent silver streams, which we now see glide so quietly by us. — [*Izaak Walton.*

Abused mortals, did you know
Where joy, heart's-ease and comforts grow,
    You'd scorn proud towers,
    And seek them in these bowers,
Where winds, sometimes, our woods perhaps may shake,
But blust'ring care could never tempest make,
    Nor murmurs e'er come nigh us,
    Saving of fountains that glide by us.
                  — [*Charles Cotton.*

TABLE OF CONTENTS.

Chapter I.
                                                                             PAGE.

Prefatory and apologetic.............................. 1
Angling as a lasting pleasure........................ 3
The higher and lower branches of angling............ 4
Preparation, anticipation and recollection 5

Chapter II.
Angling and anglers vindicated....................... 8
Not all of fishing to fish 10
Love of angling no proof of sanctification............. 12
Unselfish courtesy..................................... 13

Chapter III.
Angling as a medicine 14
Prevention better than cure.......................... 17
The duty of recreation................................ 18

Chapter IV.
Re-stocking salmon waters in the Provinces............ 20
Causes of depletion................................... 21
What New York is doing.............................. 22
Fishing regulations in the Provinces................... 24

CHAPTER V.

	PAGE.
Fish breeding	29
What should be done to replenish American waters	32

CHAPTER VI.

Hobbies and some of their riders	35
Rarity of salmon anglers in the United States	38
Some of the experts of New Brunswick	40

CHAPTER VII.

Realization of a long-deferred hope	44
Whom I went with	46
Salmon fishing outfit	46
How we reached the Cascapedia	48
Scenery en route	49
Arrival and reception	51

CHAPTER VIII.

Our movement up the river	52
The Indian canoes and river rapids	53
Our first camp	55
Chief Justices Ritchie and Gray	56
A novel torch-light procession	58

CHAPTER IX.

Ticket-of-leave from the General	60
Abundance of trout	61

	PAGE.
My first casts for salmon	62
Effect of my first salmon rise	63
Fight with my first salmon	64
Victory	66

CHAPTER X.

All hands at work	68
A clogged reel	71
A provoking position	72
The chances against killing fish	75

CHAPTER XI.

Salmon habits	76
Do salmon feed in fresh water	77
The largest fish of the season breaks off	78
The weight of some of our fish	81
Shot at a moose	82
End of our first season	83

CHAPTER XII.

| An ancient angler's kit | 84 |

CHAPTER XIII.

| Brief tribute to a departed friend | 94 |

CHAPTER XIV.

| Second visit to the Cascapedia | 97 |
| Scenery coveted by anglers | 99 |

CHAPTER XV.

	PAGE.
Who went a-fishing	101
Invalid anglers	102
A pleasant camp	105
The Indian gaffer	106
The best time to fish for salmon	107
A delicate morsel	109
How to be comfortable in camp	110
The angling advantages of preserved waters	112
The attractions of forest solitudes	113

CHAPTER XVI.

A pleasant morning	116
Courtesy and self-sacrifice	117
Judge Fullerton as an angler	120
The Judge's first salmon	121
Dun trying to reel in a fifty-ton bowlder	123

CHAPTER XVII.

Difference in the play of fish	126
A pleasant disappointment	128
The wisdom of judicious commendation	129
Instances of mistakes in gaffing	130
How to treat leaping salmon	131
The music of the reel-click	132

CHAPTER XVIII.

The attractions of fly-fishing	135

	PAGE.
Trout fishing in salmon waters	136
Sea trout and brook trout	137
"Do Fish Hear?"	138
Arrival of Gen. Arthur	139
A novel merry-making	141

Chapter XIX.

A search after solitude	143
An eccentric fish	146
An upset and its consequences	148
English anglers	150

Chapter XX.

A short essay on fly-casting	151

Chapter XXI.

The best pool on the river	159
Anglers covet pleasant surroundings	160
A forest picture	162
An upset in "Lazy Bogan"	164
A narrow escape	166

Chapter XXII.

Going up the river	168
A thunder storm	170
Our champion match-lighter	171
The early morning fishing theory discussed	172
Running the rapids	174

Chapter XXIII.

	PAGE
At the Forks	176
A long fight with a gamy fish	178
A salmon quadrille	179
Patience rewarded	181
A torch-light view of the salmon pools	182

Chapter XXIV.

Forest game	187
A bear chase	188
Shot at a moose	190
A gold-seeker	191
A word about fishing tackle	192

Chapter XXV.

Leaving camp	196
A bit of rhapsody	198
Forest life not adapted to all temperaments	201
A primitive people	203
Homeward bound	204

Chapter XXVI.

Trout fishing in the Adirondacks in 1873	207
The best times to fish	209
Trolling as a pastime	210
The North Woods as a State park	211
Why anglers avoid a crowd	212

	PAGE
Martin's	213
Invalids in the woods	214
A late spring makes late fishing	215
The high dam at Setting-Pole rapids	217

Chapter XXVII.

Trolling on the lower Saranac	219
The pleasures of exploration	220
Eccentricities of memory	222
Long waiting for a wary fish	225

Chapter XXVIII.

Musings of silent men	228
A pleasant place to cast	231
Cockney fishermen	232
Trout haunts at different seasons	234
Bartlett's and Corey's	237

Chapter XXIX.

Lumbering	239
An old resident of the woods	241
Two hours' sport at "the rapids"	243
Reminiscences of Gen. Spinner	245
A fly theory exploded	247

Chapter XXX.

Setting-Pole rapids	249
A few angling reminiscences	250

Chapter XXXI.

	PAGE.
Stale fish	257
In a bad fix at Pearsefield falls	258
Capture of a four pound trout in Hitching's pond	260
The trout in Bog river and Tupper's lake	262
Notable places visited	263
Capture of a seven pound trout in Rangely lake	264
Reel up	264

First Visit to the Cascapedia.

PLEASURES OF ANGLING.

CHAPTER I.

PREFATORY AND APOLOGETIC.

To al you that ben vertuous: gentyll: and free borne I wryte and make this ſymple treatiſe folowynge: by whyche ye may haue the full craft of anglynge to dyſport you at your lufte, to the entent that your aege maye the more floure and the more longer to endure. — [*Treatiſe of Fyſſhynge with an Angle*, 1496.

WHATEVER pleasure a veteran may find in occasionally recounting his deeds of valor, the rehearsal at some time becomes monotonous. So with these talks on Angling. They were well enough years ago, but they seem to the writer thereof hardly in harmony with the assumed gravity of "furrows," "wrinkles" and "hoary locks." Not that a true angler ever passes the line which takes him into the land of ailments and decrepitude. It is the glory of the art that its disciples never grow old. The muscles may relax and the beloved rod become a burden.

but the fire of enthusiasm kindled in youth is never extinguished. The time, however, does come when one is reluctant to parade the sources of even his innocent pleasures, except, perhaps, to those " simple wise men " whom he knows to be in sympathy with him, and who can appreciate the too generally unappreciated truth that that pleasure is only worthy the pursuit of men or of angels which " worketh no evil."

But so many kind friends, who find delight in the pursuit of the gentle art, have importuned me to forego my purpose to be silent, and to permit them, just this once, to enjoy what they are pleased to characterize as " the pleasure they derive " from these rambling jottings, that I have reluctantly consented to gratify the few with whom I know I shall be *en rapport* from the start, at the hazard of displeasing the many whose highest conceptions of angling have been derived from that libelous old adage of " a rod and line, with a fool at one end and a fish at the other," and who, because of this misconception, have neither sympathy with nor respect for a recreation which the wisest and gentlest and most lovable men of all ages have recognized as the best and simplest and most effective medicine for mind and body which a kind Providence has vouchsafed erring and ailing humanity.

Although my last was my thirty-fifth annual visit to angling waters, it was anticipated with greater interest and with higher hopes of quiet enjoyment than any which had preceded it. And this, as all biography teaches, has been the experience of all true lovers of the angle. Sir Humphrey Davy retained his enthusiasm to the last. When, like Jacob, he had to lean heavily upon his staff, the author of *Noctes Ambrosiana* would wade his favorite streams with all the pleasure of his early manhood; and long after every other delight had waxed and waned, this remained as the veritable elixir of perpetual youth. "Kit North's" daughter (Mrs. Gordon) gives this charming picture of him when a hopeless invalid:

"And then he gathered around him, when the spring morning brought gay jets of sunshine into the little room where he lay, the relics of a youthful passion, one that with him never grew old. It was an affecting sight to see him busy, nay quite absorbed, with the fishing tackle about his bed, propped up with pillows—his noble head, yet glorious with its flowing locks, carefully combed by attentive hands, and falling on each side of his unfaded face. How neatly he picked out each elegantly dressed fly from its little bunch, drawing it with trembling hand across the white coverlet, and then, replacing it in his pocket-book, he would tell, ever and anon, of the streams he used to fish in of old, and of the deeds he had performed in his childhood and youth."

And the experience of the past is that of to-day — not among the eminent alone, but among the lowly as well, who find pure delight and refreshing recreation in quiet forests and by the side of crystal waters, with no other companions than rod and reel, singing birds and summer zephyrs. "As Dr. Boteler said of strawberries, 'Doubtless God could have made a better berry, but doubtless God never did;' and so, if I may be judge, God did never make a more calm, quiet, innocent recreation than Angling."

But it would be an inexcusable exaggeration to assume that this strong liking grows upon those who only engage in the grosser departments of the art. The greatest enthusiast soon wearies of bait and troll as lures for pike and pickerel, or sun fish and perch. As coarse food palls on the palate, so the love of angling soon dies out unless it reaches up to the higher plane of trout and salmon, lured by the tiny fly, kept in check by the gossamer-like leader, and conquered by the skillful manipulation of the slender rod, which curves to the pressure as gracefully as the tall pine to the blast of the tempest. It is only in this higher department of the art that the angler finds the witchery of his vocation and the octegenarian the ecstacy which gives to him ever increasing pleasure and delight. If the fascinating art had no other commendation than this, that the pleasure which it affords never abates but grows in attractiveness and intensity with every repetition, it would be worthy of cultivation, and should commend itself to all who deem it possible for old age to have some more tangible joy than that afforded by the barren recollections of the distant past.

Nor is it alone during the all too brief period in which he is actually engaged in whipping the rivers and bagging the spoil that the angler derives delight from his art. Weeks before it is practicable to visit " the woods," or proper to even attempt to "entice the finny tribe from their aqueous element," the chronic angler finds exquisite delectation in the needful preparation for his sojourn

> Where lakes and rills and rivulets do flow;
> The lofty woods, the forests wide and long.
>   Adorned with leaves, and branches fresh and green,
> In whose cool bowers the birds with many a song
>   Do welcome with their choir the Summer's Queen;
> The meadows fair, where Flora's gifts among
>   Are intermixed, with verdant grass between;
> The silver-scaléd fish that softly swim
> Within the sweet brook's crystal watery stream.

The recollection of what has been and the anticipation of what is to be; the quiet discourse of men with like tastes, of past successes and of anticipated triumphs; reminiscences of river and lake and forest and camp-fire, make up a series of prospective and retrospective pleasures akin to those experienced by the old soldier fondling his trusty matchlock and "fighting his battles o'er again."

And unpacking one's kit is like meeting old friends. Every marred fly, every frayed leader, every well-worn tip and line and reel, revives pleasant memories of river, pool or camp-fire, of "rise," or "strike," or struggle, only less real than the reality itself, for "only itself can be its parallel."

No marvel that apostles and prophets, emperors and kings, philosophers and bishops, soldiers and statesmen, scholars and poets, and the quiet, gentle and contemplative of all ages and of all professions, have found delight in angling, or that they have been made the better and the wiser, and the purer and the happier, by its practice. It brings its devotee into close and intimate communion with nature. It takes him into flowery meads and shady woods; by the side of murmuring brooks, silvery cascades and crystal rivers; through deep ravines, sentineled by cloud-clapped mountains, and into valleys clothed in vernal beauty, and made vocal with rippling waters and the warbling of feathered songsters. It would have been strange indeed if an art which requires such surroundings, and which can only be successfully practised by the exercise of patience and a quiet temper, had not been discovered by Sir Henry

Wotton to be "a rest to the mind, a cheerer of the spirits, a diverter of sadness, a calmer of unquiet thoughts, a moderator of passions, a procurer of contentedness;" or that what thus ministers medicine to the mind while it invigorates the body, should not prove attractive to all who

> Find tongues in trees, books in the running brooks,
> Sermons in stones, and good in every thing.

To many this prologue may seem as irrelevant as angling seems simple to the uninitiated; but I have been lured on by my theme as I have often been by the shady banks and singing waters beside which I have cast my fly through the long summer day, in sheer forgetfulness of time and distance and all else save the consciousness of supreme enjoyment. An angler is, from necessity, a rambler; and if he wields his pen as he makes his casts, he must needs drop his thoughts as he drops his leader, whenever and however the inspiration of the moment suggests.

CHAPTER II.

ANGLING AND ANGLERS VINDICATED.

> We care not who says,
> And intends it dispraise,
> That an angler to a fool is next neighbor.
> Let him prate; what care we;
> We're as honest as he,
> And so let him take that for his labor!
> —[*Charles Cotton.*

WHAT good Sir Izaak Walton said two hundred years ago, of those who scoff at angling as "a heavy, contemptible, dull recreation," is quite as appropriate for their successors of to-day.

"You know, gentlemen, it is an easy thing to scoff at any art or recreation: a little wit, mixed with ill-nature, confidence and malice, will do it; but though they often venture boldly, yet they are often caught, even in their own trap, according to that of Lucian, the father of the family of scoffers:

> ' Lucian well skilled in scoffing, this hath writ:
> Friend, that's your folly which you think your wit;
> This you vent oft, void both of wit and fear,
> Meaning another, when yourself you jeer!'

"If to this you add what Solomon says of scoffers, that 'they are an abomination to mankind,' let him that thinks fit scoff on, and be a scoffer still; but I account them enemies to me and to all that love angling.

"And for you that have heard many grave, serious men pity anglers, let me tell you, sir, that there are many who are taken by others to be serious and grave men, which we contemn and pity,—men that are taken to be grave because nature hath made them of a sour complexion, money-getting men, men that spend all their time first in getting and next in anxious care to keep it; men that are condemned to be rich, and then always busy or discontented; for such poor-rich men, we anglers pity them perfectly, and stand in no need to borrow their thoughts to think ourselves so happy. No, no, sir, we enjoy a contentedness above the reach of such dispositions. * * *

"And for our 'simplicity,' if you mean by that a harmlessness, or that simplicity which was usually found in the primitive Christians, who were, as most anglers are, quiet men and followers of peace—men that were so simply wise as not to sell their consciences to buy riches, and with them vexation and a fear to die; if you mean such men as lived in those times when there were fewer lawyers, when men might have had a lordship conveyed to them on a piece of parchment no bigger than your hand, though several sheets will not do it safely in this wiser age,—I say, sir, if you take us anglers to be such simple men as I have spoken of, then myself and those of my profession will be glad to be so understood; but if by simplicity you mean to express a general defect in those that profess the excellent art of angling, I hope in time to disabuse you, and make the contrary appear so evidently, that, if you will have but patience to hear me, I shall remove all the anticipations that discourse, or time, or prejudice, have possessed you against that laudable and ancient art; for I know it is worthy the knowledge and practice of a wise man."

They are greatly in error who suppose that all there is of fishing is to fish. That is but the body of the art. Its soul and spirit is in what the angler sees and feels — in the murmur of the brook; in the music of the birds; in the simple beauty of the wild-flowers which peer at him from every nook in the valley and from every sunny spot on the hill-side; in the moss-covered rock; in the ever-shifting sunshine and shadow which give ever-varying beauty to the sides and summits of the mountains; in the bracing atmosphere which environs him; in the odor of the pine and hemlock and spruce and cedar forests, which is sweeter to the senses of the true woodsman than all the artificially compounded odors which impregnate the boudoirs of artificial life; in the spray of the waterfall; in the grace and curve and dash of the swift-rushing current; in the whirl of the foaming eddy; in the transparent depths of the shaded pool where, in mid-summer, the speckled trout and silver salmon "most do congregate;" in the revived appetite; in the repose which comes to him while reclining upon his sweet-smelling couch of hemlock boughs; in the hush of the woods when moon and stars shine in upon him through his open tent or bark-covered shanty; in the morning song of the robin; in the rapid-coursing blood, quickened by the pure unstinted mountain air which imparts to the lungs the freshness and vigor of its own vitality; in the crackling of the newly kindled camp-fire ; in the restored health, and in the thousand other indescribable and delightful realities and recollections of the angler's camp-life on lake or river during the season when it is right to "go a-fishing." It is these, and not alone or chiefly the mere act of catching fish, which render the gentle art a source of constant and ever-growing pleasure. But to attain unto the full measure of delight which the pastime affords, the angler must not be merely an expert in the mechanism of the art. Unless he can, withal, appreciate the beauties of nature, and "look from nature up to nature's God," he has neither the spirit of the old masters of the angle, nor a just comprehension of its refining and elevating possibilities.

While plying his vocation in these quiet places, with no noisy babblers to break in upon his meditations, with every nerve thrilling with the intensest satisfaction, with the mind as free from rasping care as the pure atmosphere in which he is enveloped is from the miasma of the far-off lagoon, and with heart and brain in harmonious accord and sympathy with the peaceful serenity of the scene and the occasion, is it strange that sometimes he makes the old woods ring with his shouts in the very *abandon* of delight? It may not be that these raptures come to all the brethren of the angle, but they come in full measure to but few besides; because the true angler, "born so," as good Sir Izaak hath it, has within himself, more than those who have no sympathy with his craft, the elements which are necessary to bring him thus *en rapport* with Nature. And I say all this, not to elevate the art above what is becoming, but to show that the angler, in the quiet pursuit of his craft, finds other attractions, purer and higher and more ennobling, than the mere act of taking fish. Let not those who are so "of the earth earthy" as to be unable to find any other pleasure in this pastime than that derived from "striking" and "killing" their prey, write themselves down as the disciples of the quiet and gentle Father of the art. For they are "bastards and not sons," and merit a place rather among the pot-hunters of the guild than among its appreciative disciples.

But fondness for fishing is no proof of sanctification. The selfish man at home is selfish in his pleasures; and there is no pastime where one is oftener tempted to be selfish than in angling. Few, indeed, are those who would send a friend to a favorite pool before he himself had tried it. To do so is the very highest proof of magnanimity. I have known a few such in my experience — men who, if asked for their coat would give their cloak also; but they are so rare that I can count them on my fingers. There comes up before me, as I write, the grandest specimen of unselfishness, in this regard, who ever cast a fly or kindled a camp-fire. If he chanced to strike a "school," or discovered other signs of abundant sport, his cheery shout would always indicate to his companions his desire that they might share his good fortune. And this was but a type of his character. He was and still is a living illustration of the scripture assurance that it is "more blessed to give than to receive." And I have just received a note from another friend of kindred spirit, who knew no way by which he could better emphasize his appreciation of a trifling favor than to say: "It will give me great pleasure to reciprocate your kindness; and should we ever again meet in the forest, and beside a pool where the speckled beauties await our deceptive lure, I will yield it, and grant to you its undisturbed possession." And he would keep his promise; for thirty years of angling has rendered him as unselfish in his amusements as he is genial in his social life.

CHAPTER III.

ANGLING AS A MEDICINE.

Yf a man lacke leche or medicyne he fhall make thre thynges his leche and medicyne: and he fhall nede neuer no moo. The fyrfte of theym is a mery thought. The feconde is labour not outrageo. The thyrde is dyete mefurable. Fyrfte that yf a man wyll euer more be in mery thoughtes and have a glad fpyryte, he muft efchewe all contraryous company, and all places of debate where he myghte haue any occafyons of malencoly. And yf he woll haue a labour not outrageo he muft thenne ordeyne him to his hertys eafe and pleafaunce, wythout ftudye, penfyfneffe or traueyle, a mery occupacyon, which may rejoyce his herte: and in whyche his fpyrytes may haue a mery delyte. And yf he woll be dyetyd mefurably, he muft efchewe all places of ryotte whyche is caufe of furfette and fykneffe: and he muft drawe him to places of fwete ayre and hungry: and ete nourifhable meetes and dyffyable alfo. — [*Treatife of Fyffhynge with an Angle*, 1496.

CONCUR with those who speak of the pastime of angling as a medicine, not alone from my own experience, although that may count for something, but from the great number of strong men with whom I have been brought in intimate contact during my more than thirty years of outdoor life, and who, from their youth up, have found nothing so invigorating as the pure air of the mountains; nothing so soothing, after the toil and worry and fret of business, as the silence of the woods; nothing so pervading in its mellowing influence upon nerve and brain and spirit as the pleasant murmur of the flowing river; nothing so health-giving as the aroma of nature's grand forest laboratory; and nothing so exhilarating as the rise and swirl and rush of trout or salmon. Those whom I have thus known, with scarcely an exception, have preserved the vigor of lusty youth longer and more uniformly than their contemporaries who have sought other means of recuperation and other sources of enjoyment;—from which I infer either that few but those who are blest with robust constitutions ever acquire a passion for angling, or that the pastime itself creates the healthful vitality which insures a vigorous old age. But whether the pastime is merely preservative or is really curative in its medicinal effects, it is certainly beneficent, and deserves the high place it holds in the affections of its happy, healthy and enthusiastic votaries.

However angling may be classed by others — whether as a fool's pastime or as a wise man's recreation — I have always found great pleasure in recognizing what its indulgence costs me as so much saved from my doctor's bill. And as my doctor, who passed his seventy-fifth year before "the grasshopper became a burden," was himself a life-long disciple of the gentle art, he never chided me for my tastes nor coveted what was kept from him by their indulgence. And now, when this "beloved physician" is "wearing awa' to the land o' the leal" as gently and as peacefully as the summer's sun retires to its rosy couch, his eye receives new lustre as he recalls the pleasant hours of his early youth while angling in the lochs and burns of his native land and in the brooks and rivers of his adopted country.

And just here is where too many of our people make their great mistake. They seek recreation to regain health, not to preserve it. If half the time were given to keep strong that is consumed in the hopeless effort to get strong, there would be fewer invalids in the land — fewer men prematurely aged, and fewer women bent and broken in the midst of their years. "Prevention is better than cure," and no class of men are more fortunate than those whose love of angling frequently draws them from the wearisome cares of business and the suffocating atmosphere of absorbing trade, into the green fields and shaded forests, where brook and river and lake afford ample pastime and healthful recreation.

I think our people are improving in this regard. There are more who appreciate the curative properties of change and repose to-day than ever before; and the time is coming when the expenses of a brief vacation, whether to hamlet or palace, to lake or river, to forest or sea-shore, to valley or mountain, will enter into every one's calculations as regularly as any other of the necessaries of life. If, as some allege, Americans have degenerated in muscular development and in general *physique*, it may be attributed to their intense and unceasing application to business, rather than to any thing deteriorating in our climate. It is quite as true of the worker, whether of brain or of muscle, who never gives himself a day's real rest in a score of years, as it is of the wicked, "that he shall not live out half his days." Those who deliberately and from a settled purpose to get gain at any cost, wear themselves out prematurely, are foremost among "the wicked" referred to; and the admonition is for their benefit quite as much as for the epicure or debauchee.

I remember, many years ago, while "lying round loose" for a few days at Lebanon, meeting a friend who accosted me with, "Why, D., what are you doing here? I had not heard you were ailing, and supposed you enjoyed perfect health." "Yes," I replied, "thanks to a kind Providence, I am never really sick, and to-day I am as free from ailment as a sky-lark from bronchitis." "Well, I am glad to hear it, certainly; but if you are perfectly well, why are you here?" "To keep well, judge." I will never forget the shadow of sadness which crossed his care-worn countenance as he replied: "Yours is the true philosophy. I have been working very hard for thirty years, and this is my first vacation; and I am here now, not from choice but from necessity. My doctor tells me I have impaired my constitution by over-work, and that my only hope is rest. But I fear I have postponed this rest too long. You and those like you, who will have your recreation whatever becomes of business, are the wisest men. You rest to preserve health and not to regain it. I am seeking what, by my too close application to business, I have prematurely lost; and it is very doubtful whether I shall find what I am seeking." And his fear was prophetic. He died in the midst of his years — a man exemplary in all things save in this neglect of himself. And for this he paid the inevitable penalty.

It is a sorry sight to see an over-worked, sallow-visaged, prematurely aged man of business, voluntarily digging his own grave. Yet thousands are doing this, because they will not seek rest until their accumulations will permit them to "retire" to enjoy what they have "made," and when such men do "retire," they find themselves possessed of a fortune and a broken constitution. Who, then, are the wise men? They who work without cessation or intermission until they are compelled to seek lost health, or they who prefer "prevention" to "cure?" If to merely "work" was all of life, even then would it be economy to spend an occasional month in the woods; for here the muscles as well as the brain and the heart find recuperative aliment. The scripture hath it: "He that maketh haste to be rich shall not be innocent"—not that he always does wrong to his neighbor, but that he too often and most inexcusably does wrong to himself.

But angling is not alone a health-retaining and a health-giving pastime. It is a medicine to the mind as well as to the body; and unlike too many of the pleasures of life, it scatters no seeds from which the nettle of remorse may grow to sting the conscience or drive sunshine from the heart. Like the unclouded friendships of youth, it leaves only joyous memories. Peter did not weep because he took fish with net or angle, but because he did what it has become a proverb no angler can do and have "luck," and if Uncle Toby's hasty speech had been as free from guile as an angler's heart while plying his vocation, no angel's tear need to have fallen to blot out the record. Blessed pastime, whose day never ends, but whose sun casts a perpetual radiance upon the "simple wise man" who, regularly as the return of "the time of the singing of birds," sayeth to himself, "I go a-fishing!"

We thank God, therefore, for these woods, these mountains and these ever-singing waters. They are not only the angler's Elysium, but the great medicine chest of nature.

CHAPTER IV.

RE-STOCKING SALMON WATERS — WHAT HAS BEEN AND WHAT MAY BE.

There's a river in Macedon, and there is also, moreover, a river in Monmouth; it is called Wye at Monmouth, but it is out of my prains what is the name of the other river; but 'tis all one, 'tis so like as my fingers is to my fingers, and there is salmons in both.—[*King Henry V.*, *Act* 4, *sc.* 7.

HE longing of twenty years has been gratified. I have had three weeks' salmon fishing in one of the best rivers on the continent; and as many of my readers are quite as fond of angling as I am myself, they will be interested in a brief record of my experience in this highest department of the gentle art.

All the most desirable salmon rivers in the three provinces of Quebec, New Brunswick and Nova Scotia, are preserved. Not many years since it became alarmingly apparent that this kingly fish was being rapidly exterminated, and that, unless some stringent measures were adopted for its preservation, it would speedily become as scarce as it had heretofore been abundant. The experience of the past sixty years furnished a melancholy lesson of the danger of neglect. For within that period, every stream, as far south as the river Credit (at the head of lake Ontario) and on both sides of that lake, lake Champlain and the St. Lawrence river down to Quebec, were as prolific in salmon as any of the rivers on the gulf or on the coast of Labrador. I myself remember when canoe-loads of salmon were brought to Toronto from the first-named river by the Indians and sold for a penny a pound; and it is within the recollection of the "oldest inhabitants" of Sodus, Oswego, Kingston, Prescott and Plattsburg, when salmon in the rivers in their neighborhood were quite as plenty as salmon trout, white fish or black bass now are. But now, a salmon in any of the waters south of Montreal is as rare as a Spanish mackerel north of the Highlands in the Hudson.

This depletion has resulted from three causes: 1. The destruction of the fish by net and spear; 2. The establishment of saw-mills and factories; and 3. The erection of dams which prevent the fish from resorting to their natural breeding places. Either of these causes would, in time, perform the work of extermination; but the latter is the most effective and the least excusable, because unnecessary. A very little attention to the construction of "ladders" to enable the fish to reach their spawning beds would have insured their annual return without at all impeding "the march of improvement." But this simple provision was neglected (if thought of), and what with the net and spear and the poisonous substances introduced into the waters, the places which once knew the salmon in the greatest profusion will now know them no more forever — unless, indeed, the more perfect knowledge we now have of what is needful to restore the waste places on our inland waters shall be brought into practical use by individual enterprise or by governmental interposition.

Something is being done in this direction by our own State, but so parsimoniously and upon so petty a scale that very little can be accomplished. Our legislators, however, may do better as they grow wiser, although our inland fisheries may never become what they have been. There are difficulties in the way which neither care, science nor liberality can overcome. But enough may be accomplished, at a cost which would be voted a mere bagatelle when contrasted with the results, to bring back to the waters of our State a moderate abundance of this delicious fish, for which we are now dependent, for the most part, upon the distant provinces of Quebec, New Brunswick and Nova Scotia. Indeed, even though New York should continue to creep in the laggard way in which she has begun, there is still hope that something may be achieved in restoring salmon to the streams flowing into lake Ontario. The Upper Canada government has authorized two or three breeding establishments west of Kingston, and they have been so carefully and so wisely supervised by its agent (a Mr. Wilmot), that the very best results are foreshadowed. Several streams have been stocked, and already thousands of young fish, which were hopefully cast upon the waters, have, with that curious and mysterious instinct which is as unerring as the sun, returned to vindicate their sagacity and to encourage the agents of the government in their beneficent labors. If our own State authorities shall be equally wise and quadruple the powers and resources of our intelligent fish commissioners, the next generation may not be able to buy salmon for a penny a pound, but they will be procurable in such abundance as to render them as available as white fish or shad.

It was this experience of the past sixty years, and the recollection of the total depletion of the once prolific streams emptying into the upper St. Lawrence and lake Ontario, which impressed the authorities of the three lower Provinces with the necessity of enacting some stringent laws to prevent their own waters from becoming equally "barren and unfruitful." The first step was to declare all the rivers (with a few exceptions) closed to all comers not duly authorized to fish there by the proper authorities. Then followed the appointment of a commission of fisheries — one commissioner for each province. These officials are given the general supervision of all the inhibited rivers — issuing licenses to those who are permitted to fish with seines in tide-water, and leases to those who wish the rivers for purely angling purposes. The prices paid for licenses for seine-fishing vary with the presumed prolific character of the fishing grounds, from $100 to $500; and so of the rivers leased to anglers, varying from $100 to $600. The latter is the annual sum paid by the lessee of the Cascapedia, where I have had my first experience in salmon fishing. The seines are not to obstruct the entire of the channel in any river, and ordinarily do not cover more than one-tenth of the water surface; so that, while many fish are caught, as is proper, ten times as many find an unobstructed passage to the fresh water, which they instinctively seek, with the regularity of the seasons, to breed. The leases for angling include all of the rivers lying above tide-water, and restrict the lessee to hook and line. Spearing and all other modes of fish-taking (except with the fly) are prohibited under penalties which would be deemed severe were they not indispensable to the preservation of the waters from voracious pot-hunters and inveterate poachers. Each river has a warden, appointed by the fish commissioners or lessee, and are paid a moderate stipend (from $50 to $250) jointly by the government and the lessee. This warden designates trustworthy parties in the neighborhood as watchers, who are stimulated to a careful discharge of their duties by the lion's share of the penalties which may be imposed upon the violators of the law. By these means, the rivers are, as a general thing, well preserved — so well that it is the verdict, not only of the authorities but of the most intelligent residents on the preserved streams, that the salmon are to-day many times more numerous than they were before the rivers passed under the supervision of their wardens. This testimony was more especially given in regard to the Cascapedia, where I fished.

The inhibition is, of course, distasteful to the people, who have heretofore had free access to these rivers; and they are not slow to give expression to their feelings. Indeed, one must have a profound reverence for the law or an intense terror of its penalties, who, with a scant larder, can witness a dozen salmon leaping from the pool in front of his log cabin, without either "casting" for them or anathematizing the law which prevents him from doing so. A free and independent "Yankee" would no more brook such an interference with his rights, or think of going to bed hungry with such an appetizing morsel impudently flopping his tail at him, than he would of turning either the back of his hand to a friend or the back of his coat to an enemy. And this, not because he would be oblivious of the propriety of preserving the fish from extermination, but because he would demonstrate to his own satisfaction not only that "self-preservation is the first law of nature," but that "necessity knows *no* law," and that when salmon thus generously say to him, "Come and take me," no government has a right to say, "You shan't do it." Superadded to this would be the antagonism excited by the reflection that, in this case, the prohibition is against nature and the right which every man has to the waters and all that is therein in front of his own premises. Many even here, who are not Yankees, believe that if this right were asserted it would hold good — unless it had been voluntarily surrendered or otherwise legally secured by the government. Fortunately, however, on most of the salmon rivers, the government is the principal owner of the lands on either side of them; and where it is not, if the question were raised, some mode would be devised to effect the beneficent ends sought by this law of inhibition, without wholly ignoring this ancient right.

So far as the people here are concerned, they

seem to generally acquiesce (though not without grumbling) in the law as entirely within the province of the government and as promotive of the best good of the greatest number. That there is frequent poaching, the local court records furnish abundant evidence. The flambeaux and spear have been too long in use and have too long afforded both sport and provender to be all at once abandoned. But no mercy is shown to those who are caught. A heavy fine, ranging from $5 to $50 and the forfeiture of the canoe with its contents, are the sure penalty of those found repeating the offense. The whites bear it with the meekness and patience becoming the law-loving subjects of her gracious majesty; but when "Lo, the poor Indian" finds himself mulcted in damages and robbed of his canoe (which is at once his lumber wagon and his coach-and-four) he gives vent to something more emphatic if not more expressive than a sigh for the good old days when he was "boss" of the continent.

The prohibition, however, does not extend to trout — which abound in all the salmon rivers to an extent which would render each one of them a distinct and separate paradise to the trout angler. Any resident on the preserved rivers may fish for trout; and if, while thus engaged, they have the misfortune to hook a salmon, I have never heard of an instance where he was shaken off as an intruder. In such a case, the offense, I believe, is generally forgiven by the warden if reported to him. That a great many are thus taken (always accidentally, of course,) there is no doubt. But these occasional mistakes have no perceptible effect upon the run of the fish, and are wisely winked at by those whose duty it is to see that no salmon goes into the pickle-barrel without first paying tribute to the Queen.

CHAPTER V.

WHAT THE PROVINCES ARE DOING, AND WHAT NEW YORK SHOULD DO.

That which is good to be done cannot be done too soon; and if it is neglected to be done early, it will frequently happen that it will not be done at all.—[Bishop Mant.

I CAN pay the Provincial authorities no higher compliment than to say that, so far as I am able to judge, they never do things by halves. What they deem it necessary to do, they deem it wise to do well. This is a good rule for all governments not only, but for all individuals as well. The world has lost at least a century in achievement, because so much that has been attempted has lacked the stamp of thoroughness in its prosecution. "A lick and a promise" is the homely adage sometimes applied to the imperfect results of slip-shod labor. The intelligent observer has daily cause to deplore the fallibility of human nature when he contrasts the golden promises with the leaden performances of men in authority. If all that kings and presidents, and cabinets and congresses, from the days of Charlemagne until now, have decreed *should be* had come to pass, the millenium would have been at least as old as our republic, and government defaulters and lecherous scandal-mongers would have been as scarce as chub in a salmon pool. But, unfortunately, only a beggarly moiety of what was promised ever found embodiment in performance, and most of what was attempted, looking to the amelioration and elevation of the race, was prosecuted so feebly — with so little of the essential element of thoroughness — that the devil has seldom had occasion to thrust out his cloven foot to stop the car of progress.

By which digression I simply mean to say, that when the Provincial authorities determined to preserve their salmon fisheries, they determined to make thorough work of it — to replenish as well as to preserve — not only to guard what came to them in a natural way, but to avail themselves of all the artificial processes which practical science had developed. Hence, besides fish commissioners and fish wardens and a fish police, they recognize and employ fish breeders — men of experience, intelligence and integrity (alas! what a rarity) to whom they give *carte blanche* (as unrestricted as that given to Adam) to go forth and replenish the waters with this king of fish and rarest morsel that ever melted on a gourmand's palate.

And this is being done — not (as in New York) by a beggarly contribution to a petty hatching-house which one might cover with a good sized Mexican sombrero, situated so remote from the natural haunts of the most valuable fish sought to be propagated that it requires even more care and skill to transport the tender fry where they are needed than it does to catch them after they are full grown. These provincial establishments are placed where nature has placed a man's nose — just where they are needed, and just where, like the gratuitously distributed Pacific railroad stock, they can "do the most good" — on the natural salmon rivers, where the raw material is at hand (this is not intended as a pun upon the mode of manipulation), and where the product, like all good deeds cast upon the world's waters, will "return after many days," to fill the nets of the fisherman, the exchequer of the realm, and the pickle-barrel (and stomach) of the consumer. If, as is the case, the spawn or fry is needed for remote waters, either to introduce or to replenish, they are quite as available for this purpose as if, as at our State hatching-house, the raw material had to be imported before it can be dispensed — with the single exception of brook trout, which are as indigenous to Caledonia brook as salmon are to the Cascapedia.

These provincial hatching-houses, like the salmon

fry which they are to furnish, are still in their infancy. Only two or three are yet erected; but the work is going on, and in a very few years there will be one or more on every principal salmon river in the three provinces. Mr. Wilmot, the son of the gentleman who began the business on lake Ontario several years since, has charge of them, and from what I saw of him during my recent visit, I am quite sure that he is the right man in the right place.

I have said this much on this subject of fish breeding, not because I object to what has been done at home, but with the earnest hope that what I have said or shall say may stimulate our legislature to do more. Our fish commissioners have done well with the scanty means placed at their disposal, and Seth Green, their zealous and intelligent agent, deserves the thanks and gratitude of the whole people. But you might as well try to scoop out lake Ontario with a landing net as to properly replenish our barren waters with the fish natural to them from the product of the all too limited establishment at Mumford.

We are mercifully told that Providence winked at what was done foolishly "in the time of man's ignorance." And while legislators were confessedly and excusably "ignorant" of the results of fish-breeding, no one was disposed to find fault with their excessive parsimony. But this time of excusable ignorance is past; and now the man who does not comprehend the grand possibilities of fish-breeding, and who is unwilling to give his vote for its extension, is quite unfit to represent an intelligent constituency, and is himself a — well, a fish which is far less attractive to an artistic eye than to an epicurean palate. The Mumford hatching-house and its zealous manipulator have returned to the State and country a thousand fold for all they have expended. But "the little-one" should "become a thousand." From having the only source of supply so diminutive and so obscurely located that a stranger would waste as much time in discovering its whereabouts as Diogenes did in his vain search for an honest man, Seth Green should be made the superintendent of State hatching-houses at a dozen points in the Adirondacks, on lake Ontario, on the Hudson, and on several other waters, so that fish might be made a source of as great wealth to the State and of as great benefit to the people as the hog and poultry crop combined.

Anglers may be deemed a useless race by men who haven't juice enough in their composition to perspire with the thermometer at 90, nor muscle enough in their right arm to cast an eight ounce fly rod; but if their love of the sport and their desire, in season, to be able to effectively cast their lines in pleasant places, shall result in such an enlightenment of the people and in such a concentration of public sentiment as to compel such wise and liberal legislation as will insure the replenishment of all our depleted streams with the fish indigenous to them, they will deserve the benedictions of all who would much rather feast and fatten upon the toothsome flakes of trout and salmon than grow lean and cadaverous in sipping the imaginary "nectar of the gods."

I find myself drawing toward my theme as a prudent general invests a beleaguered city, by very gradual approaches. But few fish are more prolific than the salmon, and those who write about them should be excused if in this they are like them. Besides, the salmon is the king of fish, and all kings have many subjects. And still besides,—a salmon pool can only be fished successfully when approached with caution. I am acting upon this principle in penning these rambling chapters. I do not intend to hazard the satisfaction I find in composing them, or the diversion which awaits those who shall have the good taste to read them, by any premature denouement. Half the pleasure of the "good times" of life is lost by the rush and hurry with which they are begun and ended. Just now, for the first time in half a century, I am in no hurry. It is a new sensation and I rather like it.

CHAPTER VI.

HOBBIES AND SOME OF THEIR RIDERS.

> The variety and contrary choices that men make in the world argue that the same thing is not good to every man alike. This variety of pursuits shows that every one does not place his happiness in the same thing.—[*Locke.*

IT is not true that "every man has his hobby." The great mass of men have no special source of pleasurable diversion. They are content to walk the weary treadmill of life in stoical monotony, if they can but have the barren assurance that "their oil and their wine increaseth." But with the man who has his "hobby" it is not so. Equally with others, he has respect unto his larder and his bank account, and is as willing as the most thoroughly devoted man of business to have "both ends meet" seasonably and symmetrically. He has no less zeal or energy, and is quite as industrious and thrifty as his neighbor; but through the rift in the cloud of his daily struggle, he catches frequent glimpses of his beloved "hobby," and his heart throbs and his step becomes elastic as the hour approaches when he can "take a ride." It may be that the "hobby" is trotted out daily in the form of a rose-bud, a sheet of music, the framework of some impracticable piece of mechanism, an unsolvable problem in mathematics, or a newly-devised "fly," lovingly fondled in anticipation of its grand achievements upon some remote sunny holiday, when the dear "hobby" shall prance by the side of a murmuring meadow brook or a babbling mountain rivulet. However, wherever or whenever ridden, (whether with every sunset or with the waning moon, or only once a year when trout and salmon are in season,) it is well to have a harmless "hobby" standing in some cozy nook of the imagination, to be led out at will, and to be straddled and ridden when the muscles ache, when the brain is weary and when the heart is sad. The man without a "hobby" may be a good citizen and an honest fellow, but he can have but few golden threads running through the web or woof of his monotonous existence.

Of all the "hobbies" known to advanced civilization, none is more harmless, none more exhilarating, none more healthful and none which ambles more gently than that of the angler. The months of grooming — of anticipation and of preparation — are only less delightful than the pleasurable emotions experienced when, fully mounted, the happy rider " whips " his way through trout-brook and salmon-pool, buoyant in spirit, inhaling new life and vigor with every breath of the pure mountain air which environs him, with his heart pulsating as if every drop of blood was an electric battery, with every nerve thrilled by the rush and swirl preluding the coveted "strike," with the well-poised line, tensioned by the "pull" of a twenty pound salmon, droning out æolian music, and with every nerve and fibre thrumming an accompaniment, embodying more of entrancing melody than ever Strauss or Paganini dreamed of. With such a "hobby," susceptible of exciting such pleasurable emotions, upon which to take an occasional ramble through "the green pastures and beside the still waters" of life, should it be deemed strange that anglers are merry men, contemplative philosophers and enthusiasts in their love of all that is grand and beautiful and sublime in nature?

I am glad to know that the number who ride this harmless "hobby" is constantly increasing. When men through eleven months of weary toil and labor can find pleasure in anticipating the coming of the month " of all the year the best," when they will find inexpressible delectation in admiring the graceful movements of the swaying forest, in reposing beneath its genial shades, in listening to the music of bird and brook and mountain torrent, and in casting for speckled trout or silver salmon in pool or rivulet, they will not err who write them down as happier men than their neighbors, and as all the better for this happiness.

There is enough in the minor departments of angling to render it attractive. Sea and lake, as well as brook and river, afford pleasant pastime, but salmon fishing is confessedly the highest round in the ladder, whether because of the great weight, strength and beauty of the fish, the skill required to lure it to the fly, to strike it when lured, or to kill it when struck. No other fish is so shy, so kingly, or so full of game. To kill a thirty or forty pound salmon, is to graduate with all the honors. If but a comparatively few Americans, masters of every other department of the art, have attained unto this coveted dignity, it is from want of opportunity rather than from want of skill. We have no salmon rivers within our territory (where the fish will take the fly) this side the Rocky Mountains. Hence the great mass of our anglers, however skilled and enthusiastic, have deemed themselves to have reached the greatest available elevation in the art when they have killed a four, six, eight or ten pound trout. The single step forward can only be taken by a journey to Oregon or California, or by a trip to the Coast of Labrador or the Gulf of the St. Lawrence, where the restrictions are such that only a fortunate few are able to gratify their ambitious longings. There are probably not more than a dozen men in the State of New York, outside the city, who have killed a salmon. I can remember but a single person in our immediate neighborhood, beside myself, who has been so fortunate. DEAN SAGE, late of Cohoes, a young gentleman of rare skill with rod and reel and a most enthusiastic angler, had his first fortnight on a salmon river in July. It was a fortnight of exquisite pleasure, the recollection of which will make the present summer ever memorable in his log-book of years. There are, perhaps, a score or two in New York, and as many more scattered from Portland to New Orleans, who know what it is to be electrified by the "rise" of a thirty pound fish. But the number is annually increasing, and a great multitude in the next generation — if salmon breeding is pushed as it should be — will be able to enter into the feelings of grand old Christopher North when he gently caressed his pet salmon-fly on his death-bed.

It is different in the Provinces. There are enthusiastic salmon fishers in every town, from Toronto to Halifax. It was my great pleasure, during my recent visit to St. John, to form the acquaintance of some of the best of them. And I found them to be just what all true anglers ought to be, and what most true anglers are, large-hearted merry men, kindly natured, robustly gentle, hospitable as dame nature amid whose grandeur and beauty and repose they hold their annual revels. intelligent and obliging, full of enthusiasm, and so open-hearted and open-handed as to captivate and charm all who are made the delighted recipients of their hospitality.

Foremost among this bevy of gentlemen I may mention Chief Justice RITCHIE, no less respected for his virtues than honored for his learning, whose more than three score years, because of his constant walks and wanderings as an angler, have failed to check his elasticity or dampen his enthusiasm. I have pleasant camp memories of this venerable angler — of his genial *abandon*, of his pleasant jest, of his exhaustless fund of anecdote and incident, of his hearty laugh — a laugh so hearty as to give the world assurance of an honest man, and of that robust health which is the inseparable companion of what an eccentric Scotch philosopher deemed the only requisites of true felicity, viz : "a clear conscience and open bowels" — uttering no word which might not be spoken in the home circle, and yet overflowing with mellow hilarity. Happy Province which has such a Chief Justice, and happy Chief Justice who has a constituency who do not believe that he either compromises his dignity or soils his ermine by annually " going a-fishing ! "

Gen. WARNER, the American Consul, another St. John gentleman, is equally fond of rod and reel. He holds his office as the reward of faithful and intelligent service in field and forum. His appointment was as deserved as it is popular. By the wise and prudent manner in which he administers the duties of his office, he vindicates the sagacity of those who selected him for the position he honors. He is respected alike and equally by all Americans who have occasion to call upon him in his official capacity and by those who have had the good fortune to enjoy the elegant hospitality of his happy home. Although bearing an "empty sleeve"— the badge of valor and gallant service — he is an expert angler, whose love of the sport made him the lessee of the river we fished, and whose achievements with the rod and reel bear honorable comparison with those of the most accomplished of his compeers.

Mr. NICHOLSON, another member of the honorable guild, took his first lessons in angling in the lakes of Killarney, and no man is now more successful in "enticing the wary salmon to his barbed hook." If the records of his wonderful scores sometimes excite a doubt in the mind of the novice, it is a real pleasure to "make no sign," the stories are told with such infinite gusto and good humor. For my own part, I received in perfect faith every recital of his achievements — even that of the two hundred and six salmon killed in three weeks last year, and of the one hundred and twenty-two killed in half the time last June. That of a year ago was a wonderful catch — probably unsurpassed by any thing which ever before passed into the angling records of either the old world or the new.

Mr. FORBES does honor to old Harvard, whether as a barrister or as an angler. But his virtues shine out most conspicuously in his friendly offices and courteous bearing. If, as I have no doubt, he is as attentive to the interests of his clients as he is to the comfort of his friends, he should gather a rich harvest from his profession.

Mr. SPURR is the veteran angler of St. John. He has fished in all waters for twenty years, and knows more of the haunts and habits of the salmon than any other man in the province. He is a walking encyclopedia, and finds no greater pleasure than in dispensing his accumulated wisdom to those who are anxious to learn. It was fitting, therefore, that he should have taken the champion fish of the season — a forty-eight pounder — the grandest trophy attainable to mortal fisherman. It was a well-meant compliment, uttered by the unfortunate punster of our party, when he said: "This noble fish shall *Spurr* me on to a still grander achievement."

Messrs. HANFORD and ROLF and SMITH and HEADLEY and CENNET, and still others whose names but not whose good offices are forgotten, constitute a coterie of anglers and gentlemen (synonyms usually,) of whom any city might be proud, and whom it will always be a pleasure to remember.

CHAPTER VII.

WHO WENT A-FISHING, AND HOW THEY REACHED THE RIVER.

> I now believed
> The happy day approach'd, nor were
> My hopes deceived.
> — [*Dryden*.

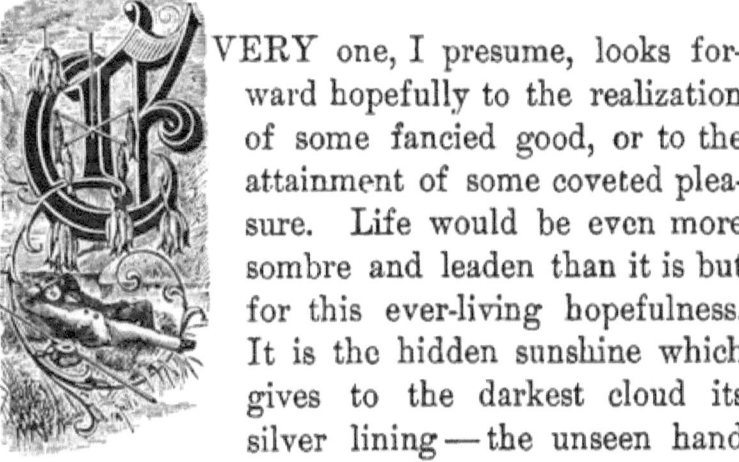

EVERY one, I presume, looks forward hopefully to the realization of some fancied good, or to the attainment of some coveted pleasure. Life would be even more sombre and leaden than it is but for this ever-living hopefulness. It is the hidden sunshine which gives to the darkest cloud its silver lining — the unseen hand which "smoothes the wrinkled front of weary care." No matter that these pleasant visions seldom assume the form and substance of reality. "Castles in the air" have often happier tenants than those on terra firma.

The enthusiastic angler is never content with minor achievements. His constant expectation is that every new cast will afford him some new conquest, and that the grand sport of to-day will be excelled by the grander sport of to-morrow. Of no others can it be said more truthfully:

"Hope springs eternal in the human breast;"—

hope not merely to capture the best of the fish for which he is angling, but hope that at some time not far off he may capture his proper quota of the gamiest fish that swims. During many more than a score of years I have found great pleasure in angling for trout, but at no time in all these years have I ceased to hope that sometime in the golden future kind fortune would favor me with the opportunity to kill a salmon. And at length, after many years of "hope deferred," the opportunity came, the excursion was projected, the waters were reached, the cast was made, hope became fruition and the coveted result was achieved. A great many pleasurable "first times" are jotted upon the memory of every one — the merchant's first successful venture, the lawyer's first case and the politician's first triumph—but none of these, nor all of them combined, can compare with the delight which comes to the enthusiastic angler from the rise and swirl and strike and capture of his first salmon. I speak from experience, and propose, for the delectation of those who are still hoping, to enter into particulars, not of that single incident alone, but of the many incidents which made our three weeks' sojourn on the Cascapedia delightfully enjoyable.

I owe to Gen. ARTHUR, Collector of the Port of New York, the opportunity of experiencing what will be "a joy forever." For several years that gentleman has given his summer vacations to salmon fishing. There are few more expert anglers and none who have a higher appreciation of the gentle art. His scores have always indicated skill and perseverance — the two essentials of success. The party, of which the General was Chief, consisted also of R. G. DUN, of New York, D. ARCHIE PELL, of Staten Island, and the writer hereof. Mr. DUN, like the General, had had several years' successful experience. Col. PELL (like his honored father before him) had had large practice in every other department of angling. But, with myself, he was about to try his "'prentice han'" on salmon waters and to make his first cast for his diploma as a graduate in the high school of the craft. I could not have fallen into better hands, nor have been brought into the association of gentlemen in more perfect accord and sympathy in all hopeful anticipation of the great pleasure in reserve for us.

The outfit for salmon fishing, though somewhat expensive if of the best — and the best, in strength if not in beauty, it always should be — is both compact and simple, consisting of a rod (costing anywhere from $35 to $60 in New York, or from $15 to $30 in St. John), an India-rubber reel ($15), an oil-boiled silk line, 300 or 400 feet in length ($8 to $12), a dozen double gut leaders with single gut droppers ($6), five or six dozen assorted salmon flies ($6 a dozen in New York or less than half that price in St. John), and a steel gaff ($2). The rods and lines may be duplicated if "expense is no object;" but only by some unforeseen accident or inexcusable carelessness need either the one or the other give out. No one is more merciless with rod and line than myself, and yet neither failed me during our expedition. Instances of failure, however, to some of the party (but not from any want of skill) occurred, and under circumstances which sorely tried the saintly tempers of these unfortunate victims of misplaced confidence. But as a rule, any strain beyond what a moderately well made rod will bear safely would almost certainly result in the loss of your fish; and the oiled line, if not imperceptibly defective, has the capacity to resist five times the pressure which should ever be employed to kill a salmon. Its great weight is given to it, not to render it secure merely, but rather to adapt it the better for casting.

In regard to supplies, whatever is needful can be better secured, and much more moderately, at Quebec or St. John than at any point this side the line. But what may be deemed "needful" depends entirely upon the tastes and appetites of the prospective consumers. One gentleman whom we met took, with himself and two guides, in a single canoe, all that he considered "needful" for a thirty days' sojourn, while another loaded two canoes, besides the one he occupied himself, with what he thought "needful" for a fortnight's excursion. I can only say to whoever may be anxious on this point, as was kindly said to our party, that it is well to "live low on the river." If, however, the advice shall be as remorselessly disregarded by any of my readers who may be contemplating a trip, as it was by our commissary, I may regret it but I shall not be surprised.

In reaching any of the rivers on the Bay of Chaleur, or in that immediate neighborhood, the most direct route is by rail to St. John and Shediac and by steamboat to Dalhousie; but the journey can be pleasantly and almost as expeditiously made by steamer from Quebec. We chose the former route, and it was high-noon of the sixth day after we left New York before we pitched our tents and prepared for service. Next year, however, there will be an all-rail route most of the way, if not quite through to Dalhousie — which, by the line of travel, is full three hundred miles from St. John.

[Now, April, 1876, there is an all-rail route to

Dalhousie, via Boston, Portland, Bangor, St. John and Moncton. Early in June of this year, it is expected that a much shorter route will be open from Montreal and River du Loup, and so across to the Bay of Chaleur. This route will greatly lessen the distance to all the most noted salmon rivers in the provinces.]

There was, in the summer of 1874, a provoking loss of twenty-four hours in making this journey, as the time-tables were arranged, there being no night train between Bangor and St. John, nor between St. John and Shediac. So that, unless you started right, you were detained a night at each of these cities. But this proved no inconvenience to those who "took no note of time," for the principal hotels at Bangor and St. John are tidy, home-like and elegant. This is especially true of the hotel at St. John (the Victoria), which ranks with the best in any city. But to those whose time is limited, and who would rather spend a day on a salmon river than a month in a palace, it is not so pleasant.

Even those in a hurry find some compensation for this delay in the attractive scenery which reveals itself at frequent intervals in the journey. It is something to see the thrifty towns below Bangor and the vast quantities of lumber and logs which fill the rivers along which the road passes. It is something, also, to see the rise and fall of the tide at St. John (from forty to fifty feet), the grand scenery with which that city is environed, and to glance at the old town itself, which, in its shipping, warehouses and marts of trade, bears the impress of real enterprise and thrift. Personally I was glad of the delay, for I had before no just conception either of the commercial-like character and future possibilities of St. John nor of the prolific character of the highly cultivated farms in its neighborhood and along the eighty miles of road to Shediac. It is by no means the dilapidated city, nor is the country about it the barren and glacier-like region I had fancied. Its fogs, however, are rather frequent for comfort, and the recollection of them somewhat dampens the enthusiasm with which I might otherwise have entered upon a description, in detail, of what, between the fogs, delighted our vision.

There are a score of excellent salmon rivers on the Gulf of St. Lawrence and the bays connected therewith; but the fish in none of them excel in size (if they do in number) those of the Cascapedia — which empties into the Bay at New Richmond, a pleasant little hamlet some thirty miles distant (and on the opposite side of the Bay) from Dalhousie, where we left the steamer and took a *chaloupe*, on board of which we spent several tedious hours, vainly whistling for the wind and uttering pointless witticisms against those whose distorted mental vision permits them to speak ravishingly of the entrancing beauty of a "sea of glass." Any thing seemed preferable to the monotony of such a cruise —a storm, a hurricane, a cyclone even, would have been welcomed; any thing but the persistent rainfall which came down just in time to drench our garments though not to dampen our spirits as we disembarked at New Richmond and received " e'en a Hieland welcome" from H. R. MONTGOMERY, Esq., to whose kindly offices we were commended by those who knew how surely his hearty courtesy and genial hospitality would obliterate the recollection of any trifling mishap which might have befallen us by the way. Here, too, we met Mr. DIMMICK, the warden of the river, who had, in the most prompt and business-like manner, responded to our telegraphed request to have canoes and guides in readiness upon our arrival. Not only were they in readiness, but they glided out from the shore at our approach, each canoe (sitting like a swan upon the water) being propelled by two paddlers (an Indian and a white man) who were to accompany us during our three weeks' sojourn on the river. Our traps and persons were speedily transferred to these frail looking but wonderfully buoyant craft, when we began what proved to be the most delightful pilgrimage I ever made to any waters.

CHAPTER VIII.

OUR FIRST CAMP AND A HEARTY WELCOME.

His grace looks cheerfully and smooth this morning ;
There's some conceit or other likes him well
When that he bids " Good morrow " with such spirit.
—[*Shakspeare.*

HE bark-canoes used upon these rivers are fragile-looking but strong and buoyant. They are not only more steady and secure, in a heavy sea, than the boats used in the Adirondacks, but are capable of bearing heavier burdens. On rivers where the current is swift and the rapids heavy (as in the Cascapedia) two men are necessary to propel them up stream with safety and comfort; and even then an average of two miles an hour is considered a fair rate of speed. The boatmen sit when paddling or stand when polling, (one at each end) while the passenger makes himself very comfortable on a slightly elevated seat in the middle of the canoe.

A novel, picturesque and exciting scene was

presented as our six canoes moved off, in "Indian file," up the rapid waters of the Cascapedia. The poles used are tipped with an iron tube, and make pleasant music as they strike upon the pebbly bottom of the river in perfect time.

The afternoon was charming. The sun shone out in full lustre, but the cool breeze rendered the atmosphere inexpressibly delightful. The river is broad and its waters are as transparent as crystal. The foliage on either side was rich and varied, and the grand old hills which rise, most of the way, almost perpendicularly from the water, were clothed in gorgeous apparel. All our surroundings — the mode of conveyance, our dusky boatmen, the scenery, the object of our journey and the sport anticipated — were novel and inspiriting, and the four hours consumed in reaching our first camping ground, were four hours of unalloyed pleasure, to which the excitement of ascending the seemingly unascendable rapids largely contributed. To ascend rapids safely not only involves hard work but a quick eye and a steady hand. To allow the impetuous current to obtain a moment's advantage would whirl the frail bark out of its course in an instant, and send it flying down upon the rocks to be dashed to pieces. It is, however, far less dangerous, though harder work, to go up than to come down these rapids. And yet, during the three weeks we were on the river, a hundred rapids, in which an Adirondack boat could not have lived a moment, were passed in perfect safety. The descent is especially exhilarating. The skill with which rocks and breakers and foam are avoided or surmounted, is a source of constant wonder and admiration. To pass through the pleasurable excitement of these dashing flights is alone worth a journey to any one of the rushing rivers where this experience can be had. The sensation of "running the rapids" is unlike anything otherwise attainable. It somewhat resembles that which one experiences from the return movement of a swing in full action; but the feeling is multiplied an hundred fold. As the rapid is approached, the water is generally as smooth as glass, and the light vessel seems drawn through it with lightning speed, as if moving upon the surface of transparent oil. From this it glides — and no other word so literally expresses the movement — into, and dashes through the foaming waters with the swiftness of a locomotive — the skilled boatmen guiding their craft past the exposed and hidden rocks by an easy and quiet motion of their paddles, as securely and as gracefully as the skilled "whip" guides his horses past any dangerous obstacle which presents itself in his pathway. This running the rapids is the very "poetry of motion," and those who have never enjoyed the sensation have something very pleasurable yet in reserve.

The point selected for our first camp was eight miles from New Richmond, and in the immediate neighborhood of several of the best pools on the river. There is no desirable fly-fishing, at any season of the year, below them. Tide-water, within which seine-fishing is allowed, extends nearly up to them, and as — for some reason with which I am not sufficiently familiar to discourse — salmon do not readily, if ever, rise to a fly until they enter fresh water, it is never deemed worth while to wet your line until these pools are reached.

On arriving at our destination, we found Chief Justice RITCHIE, of New Brunswick, and Chief Justice GRAY, of Massachusetts, in camp, awaiting our arrival to move up higher in their pursuit of sport. They gave us a most cordial welcome — so cordial and so full of cheerful heartiness and good humor as to instantly dispel the reverential awe with which plain, unlearned laymen are wont to look upon such eminent expounders of law and dispensers of justice. They had doffed their ermine and bade us welcome with unlaced dignity and grace, in flannel shirts and well-worn trousers. I have already referred to the buoyant spirits and charming hilarity of the Chief Justice of New Brunswick. He seemed an embodiment of good humor, as if he lived and moved and had his being in an atmosphere of perpetual sunshine. And Chief Justice GRAY was like him in all the good qualities desirable in camp companionship. He is a man of grand physique—more than six feet high and well proportioned—and, at home, towers above the mass of his compeers in dignity and learning as he does above most men in comely stature. It was very pleasant to mark the simple enthusiasm with which these two eminent men gave us their piscatorial experiences and recounted their achievements with rod and reel. It reminded one of the grand characters of the past—of the princes, and poets, and bishops, and chancellors, and the quiet, contemplative, happy scholars and philosophers of all times—who have found their highest delectation in their pursuit of the delightful recreation of angling. It may not seem so to the plodding man of business, who deems all time wasted which does not bring golden grist to his mill; but it is nevertheless true that there have been multitudes of wise men, and good men, and happy men in all ages who, more than when honors or wealth came to them, have rejoiced when the times and seasons returned, when they could say to their friends, as Peter said to the disconsolate disciples, "I go a-fishing." Amid his deepest gloom and despondency, this great-hearted apostle fell back instinctively upon his old vocation as the only source of comfort and relief. Multitudes of other heavy hearts and aching brains have found like relief from the same source of harmless diversion.

These distinguished anglers had had grand success. It was Judge GRAY's first visit, but having had long experience in the minor departments of the art, he found but little difficulty in acquiring the higher skill which the more complicated work of salmon-fishing requires. He had numerous trophies to exhibit in proof of the success which had attended his maiden efforts, and he referred to them with as much enthusiasm and, I doubt not, with far more satisfaction, than he had ever referred to any of his most noted triumphs in the line of his profession. It is never in a spirit of mere boasting that a true angler alludes to his achievements, but because of the simple pleasure which, like the old soldier, he derives from "fighting his battles o'er again." To rehearse the incidents connected with the capture of some famous fish, is to re-experience the thrilling sensations which accompanied the feat itself. They remain, like the recollections of some pleasant spoken word, or of some beautiful picture, or of some grand scene in nature, a joyous memory forever. He is an unhappy man who has not some pleasant wells of memory to draw upon, if it be true, as some thoughtful philosopher has said, that "half the joy of old age consists in the recollection of the pleasures of youth."

A single incident in the experience of Chief Justice RITCHIE is especially worth mentioning. Near the close of a day of fine sport he struck a thirty-pound salmon, which he tried in vain to kill before nightfall. It is a herculean task, requiring the highest skill and every possible favoring opportunity, to capture such a fish. The chances are always against success at the best. But the venerable Chief found himself tied to this monster long after twilight had ceased to fall upon the face of the waters. The pool, always dark in its great depths, soon became black as a starless midnight. There were rocks on either side of him, rushing waters above him and boiling rapids below him. His line was invisible, and the only perceptible sign of life around him or before him, was the tugging and rushing of the maddened salmon fighting for his life amid the thick darkness which every where prevailed. Under any circumstances, the venerable angler would rather, a thousand times, subject himself to the merciless criticisms which a wrong judicial decision might provoke, than to lose a fish. But under the circumstances in which, at this time, he was surrounded, he would rather have taken that fish than to have been placed on the wool-sack of the United Kingdom. And yet how could it be done? It was useless for him to soliloquize, as he did, "You beggar, I'll fight you 'till sunrise before you shall beat me." Long before sunrise the fish might escape, the canoe be swamped in some merciless rapid, and the venerable Chief left stranded and dripping upon some inhospitable rock, with nothing to cheer him in his wretched loneliness but the roar of the thundering waters or the plaintive notes of the hooting night-owl. Fortunately, neither an all-night fight nor a possible shipwreck awaited him. His co-Chief Justice took in the situation as readily as he catches the point of a lawyer's brief, improvised a few flambeaux and started off to the rescue. It was a timely interposition, resulting in perfect success. The flambeaux made the surroundings of the combatants bright as day, and in due time the salmon gave up the fight, was duly gaffed and brought into camp, escorted by the first torch-light procession in which either Chief had ever before been the principal actor.

CHAPTER IX.

CAPTURE OF MY FIRST SALMON.

"An' than," continued Jock, "whan a muckle chiel o' a salmon, wi'oot time tae consider whether yer flee is for his waime or only for his mooth — whether it's made by natur' or by Jock Hall — plays flap! and by mistak' gangs to digest what he has gotten for his breakfast, but suspec's he canna swallow the line along wi' his mornin' meal till he takes some exercise!— an' than tae see the line ticht, an' the rod bendin' like a heuck, an' to fin' something gaun fra the fish up the line and up the rod till it reaches yer verra heart, that gangs *pit pat* at yer throat like a tickin' watch; until the bonnie creatur', after rinnin' up an' doon like mad, noo sulkin aside a stane to cure his teethache, then bilkin awa' wi' a scunner at the line, tryin' every dodge, an' syne gies in, comes to yer han' clean beat in fair play, and lies on the bank, sayin' 'Waes me!' wi' his tail, an' makin' his will wi' his gills an' mooth time aboot! Eh! mon! it's splendid!"—[*Norman Macleod, D. D., in "The Starling."*]

Y impatience to make my first cast and take my first salmon was so great that the hours consumed in pitching tents, unpacking stores and arranging camp generally, seemed a sinful waste of precious moments. I did not wish, of course, to take advantage of the useful industry and greater patience of my companions; but I mentally voted them over nice in their anxiety to "make things comfortable" when, in my state of mind, the only thing which seemed requisite to the supremest comfort was the capture of a salmon. With that result achieved, I felt that I could be abundantly comfortable sitting upon a bare rock at high noon munching hard tack and bacon. I must in some way have manifested my restlessness, for the General, trying to hide his kindliness under a very thin veneering of brusqueness, said to me, "D., you are of no earthly use here. I wish you would get out of the way and go a-fishing." As this remark was made several hours before we had mutually agreed to begin work, I felt some little delicacy about taking advantage of the "ticket-of-leave" offered me. But as in the language of modern theology, I had an "inner consciousness" that I really *was* of "no use" as a tent-pitcher, and had no tact as "a man of all work" in camp preparations, I soon found myself moving canoe-ward, with my salmon and trout rods strung and my nerves in a tremor in anticipation of "the good time coming" when I would no longer have to say "I never killed a salmon." I honestly meant to show my appreciation of the General's kindness by confining myself exclusively to trout waters. And my resolution was adequate to the emergency until I became weary of the slaughter I was making of one, two, three and four-pound trout, and until (after floating below the shallow water) I was "brought up all standing" by the remark of my Indian canoe-man: "Trout plenty no more. Salmon pool here. If he should rise, trout-rod no good." My first impulse was to go immediately back to camp, and I had given the order to that effect when a grunt of surprise from my swarthy friend — who could not comprehend how any one could enter a salmon pool and leave it unfished — induced me first to hesitate, then to countermand the order, and then to appease my conscience by the remark: "Well, I will make a few casts by way of practice." No sooner said than down went the anchor at the head of what I afterward learned was one of the best pools on the river. As I seized my great salmon rod — which seemed like a cedar beam after the eight-ounce switch with which I had been fishing — and began to gradually extend my cast, I felt as I suppose the raw recruit feels when he first hears the rattle of the enemy's musketry, or as some very timid men feel when, for the first time, they stand up before a great multitude of free and independent electors to entertain and enlighten them with those profound ebullitions of wisdom and those brilliant bursts of eloquence which are commonly considered the all-sufficient and matter-of-course ingredients of a stump speech. I had reached a cast of perhaps fifty feet, in a direct line, and was watching my fly as intently as ever astronomer watched the unfoldings of a newly discovered planet, when a monster head emerged from the water, and with distended jaws — disclosing his red gills so distinctly as to make his throat look, to my excited imagination, like a fiery furnace — made a dash (which seemed like the splurge of a sea-horse) for my fly. It was my duty, of course, to accept the challenge and "strike" at the right moment and so hook my fish and take the chances for the mastery. But I had no more power to "strike" than if every limb and nerve and muscle was paralyzed. My rod remained poised but motionless, and I stood gazing at the spot where the apparition appeared, in speechless amazement, while the fly — which had, for a single moment, been buried in that great open sepulchre — reappeared upon the surface quite unconscious of the terrible ordeal through which it had passed. I do not know that any one could have "knocked me down with a feather" at that particular moment; but I do know that I never before came so near "going off in a faint," or found a cup of cold water more refreshing. I had heard of those who had had the "buck fever," and I shall hereafter have more sympathy and greater respect for them, for I undoubtedly had the malady in its most aggravated form, and felt, as my astonished guide said I looked, "pale as a ghost."

But this state of ridiculous semi-stupor lasted but for a moment. The slight twitch I felt as the fly slipped from the mouth of the fish operated like the sound of a trumpet. Every nerve tingled and the blood leaped through my veins as if every drop was an electric battery. In a very few moments, however, I was myself again. I had marked the spot where the fish had risen, had gathered up my line for another cast, had dropped the fly just where I desired it to rest, when, like a flash, the same enormous head appeared, the same open jaws revealed themselves, a swirl and a leap and a strike followed, and my first salmon was hooked with a thud, which told me as plainly as if the operation had transpired within the range of my vision, that if I lost him it would be my own fault. When thus assured, there was excitement but no flurry. My nerves thrilled and every muscle assumed the tension of well tempered steel, but I realized the full sublimity of the occasion, and a sort of majestic calmness took the place of the stupid inaction which followed the first apparition. My untested rod bent under the pressure in a graceful curve; my reel clicked out a livelier melody than ever emanated from harp or hautboy as the astonished fish made his first dash ; the tensioned line emitted æolian music as it stretched and stiffened under the strain to which it was subjected; and for fifty minutes there was such giving and taking, such sulking and rushing, such leaping and tearing, such hoping and fearing, as would have "injected life into the ribs of death," made an anchorite dance in very ecstacy, and caused any true angler to believe that his heart was a kettle drum, every sinew a jews harp, and the whole framework of his excited nerves a full band of music. And during all this time my canoe rendered efficient service in keeping even pace with the eccentric movements of the struggling fish. "Hold him head up, if possible," was the counsel given me, and "make him work for every inch of line." Whether, therefore, he took fifty yards or a foot, I tried to make him pull for it, and then to regain whatever was taken as soon as possible. The result was an incessant clicking of the reel, either in paying out or in taking in, with an occasional flurry and leap which could have been no more prevented than the on-rushing of a locomotive. Any attempt to have suddenly checked him by making adequate resistance, would have made leader, line or rod a wreck in an instant. All that it was proper or safe to do was to give to each just the amount of strain and pressure it could bear with safety — not an ounce more nor an ounce less; and I believe that I measured the pressure so exactly that the strain upon my rod did not vary half an ounce from the first to the last of the struggle.

Toward the close of the fight, when it was evident that the "jig was up" and I felt myself master of the situation, I took my stand upon a projecting point in the river, where the water was shallow and where the most favorable opportunity possible was afforded the gaffer to give the struggling fish the final death-thrust, and so end the battle. It was skillfully done. The first plunge of the gaff brought him to the green sward, and there lay out before me, in all his silver beauty and magnificent proportions, MY FIRST SALMON. He weighed thirty pounds, plump, measured nearly four feet in length, was killed in fifty minutes and afforded me more pleasure than any event since — well, say since Lee surrendered. As he was thus spread out before me, I could only stand over him in speechless admiration and delight — panting with fatigue, trembling in very ecstacy, and exclaiming with good old Sir Izaak: "As Dr. Boteler said of strawberries, 'Doubtless God could have made a better berry, but doubtless God never did;' and so, if I may judge, God never did make a more calm, quiet, innocent recreation than angling."

This victory was a surfeit for the morning. With other fish in full view, ready to give me a repetition of the grand sport I had already experienced, I made no other cast and retired perfectly contented. The beautiful fish was laid down lovingly in the bottom of the canoe and borne in triumph to camp, where fish and fisher were given such hearty welcome amid such hilarious enthusiasm as was befitting "the cause and the occasion."

In the afternoon of the same day I killed a twenty-three pound salmon in the same pool in twenty minutes, having, I was sorry to learn on getting back to camp, monopolized the luck of the day, no other member of the party having had so much as a rise. But I was soon eclipsed, both in size and number — how, when, where, by whom, under what circumstances, and amid what intense excitement, I will try and describe anon.

CHAPTER X.

A FEW NOTE-WORTHY INCIDENTS.

Eh, man! What a conceit it is when ye reach a fine run, on a warm spring mornin', the wuds hotchin' wi' birds, an' dauds o' licht noos an' thans glintin' on the water; an' the water itsel' in trim order, a wee doon, after a nicht's spate, an' wi' a drap o' porter in't, an' rowin' an' bubblin' ower the big stanes, curlin' into the linn an' oot o't.—[*Norman Macleod, D. D.*

UR camp was unusually picturesque,— a well preserved lawn separated from the river by a fringe of alders, backed by a few cultivated fields attached to the cottage in our immediate neighborhood, and surrounded by lofty mountains, densely covered from base to summit with spruce, hemlock, maple and birch. Our three white tents constituted a pleasant contrast to the green sward upon which they were pitched, and our dining hall and cook-house were models of adaptability and neatness. The taste displayed in their disposition was due, first, to the military experience of Col. PELL, and secondly, to the austere habits of system, order and neatness for which the deservedly popular

Collector of the Port of New York is distinguished. A better arranged camp, combining more of good taste and comfort, never was erected upon any waters. My only objection to it was the fear that the recollection of it would hereafter render me dissatisfied with the straggling, disjointed, haphazard way in which I have always hitherto been content to camp out. A little sound judgment and good taste goes a great way toward making even a fishing camp comfortable and attractive. I have often wondered how tidy wives could bear, with such angelic patience as some of them do, the careless ways of their slovenly husbands. If, as some insist, nothing more contributes to the happiness of a household than habitual neatness, there must be at least one very happy home in our great metropolis.

On the morning of our second day on the river, all hands were ready for work. The several pools were properly divided; each resorted to the one to which he was assigned, with high hopes and confident anticipations. And the result justified all that was hoped for. Gen. ARTHUR, as was proper, led in the score, although not in weight. Mr. DUX stood next; but Col. PELL had caught the champion fish. His first salmon weighed thirty-five pounds! It was a grand achievement, and he bore his honors and good luck with becoming meekness, although he had killed his fish in twenty minutes. This despatch indicated extraordinary skill in a novice. No expert could have done better. Indeed, it is not once in a hundred times that a thirty-five-pound salmon is brought to gaff so promptly. I was content and happy with a single fish of twenty-four pounds as the result of my day's labor.

Every new day brought new pleasures and an increase of fish; but no one caught more than five in any one day, and sometimes some one's count was *nil*. But every day brought with it some special excitement or adventure, some new incident or experience to break the monotony of the camp, and to maintain the reputation of the sport as more attractive, inspiring and exciting than any other. Among them were these:

The General had been fishing with but passable success, when the monotony was broken by a leap which indicated greater weight and dimensions than anything with which he had yet been favored. With the promptness of an expert he struck at the right moment and with the exact force requisite to hook his fish strongly — a great art, which few salmon-anglers ever acquire perfectly. Then followed a struggle which justified his estimate of the weight of the fish. For more than an hour, every known appliance was used in vain to bring him to gaff. He sulked, plunged, leaped and rushed as impetuously at the end of the hour as during the first five minutes after he was hooked. He made no sign of surrender or weariness, and was in one of his worst tantrums when *the reel clogged*. Any one with less experience and persistency than the General would have "thrown up the sponge" at such a mishap; but he was equal to the emergency. The canoe was forced rapidly forward to the beach, which was fortunately unobstructed; the General leaped upon *terra firma* with the agility of an acrobat, and after an active backward and forward movement of half an hour, manipulating his line with his hand, he bagged his game, saved his tackling, and brought to camp a thirty-four-pound salmon. Not one angler in a thousand would have achieved such a victory, and he deserved the congratulations he received when the magnificent fish was formally spread out for inspection.

And to this incident there is a moral. The reel which thus clogged at the most critical moment, was made with special reference to extra heavy work, was warranted as superior to any reel which had ever found its way upon salmon waters, and cost a fabulous sum of money. But it was a delusion and a cheat — as worthless as tow string for a salmon line and the cause of harsher words with more syllables than any reel that ever passed under my disgusted inspection. A reel that "ticks like a chronometer and moves like clock-work" is all very well in a show-case; but a reel with rough and ready action and straight-forward movements, like a man with "no nonsense about him," is the reel for service. It was the last bit of work *that* fancy reel was called upon to do during our three weeks on the Cascapedia.

Another incident, equally exciting, but resulting less fortunately, happened to the General upon another occasion. He had solidly hooked a very large fish in a pool where large fish pre-eminently abound. He sulked persistently. For nearly an hour he remained as immovable as a rock. No strain which it was safe to impose upon the rod could move him. He simply wouldn't stir. Nothing is more provoking, and nothing more tries the patience of the most patient angler. The fatigue is even greater than when hooked to a fish that deems "action, action, action," quite as essential to liberty as the rhetorician declares the same qualities indispensable to effective oratory. The tension must be equally preserved, without a moment's relaxation, whatever moods the fish may assume or whatever freaks may move him. To be obliged to stand an hour thus pulling upon an immovable object, until every muscle in one's arms seems ready to come out in shreds, is about as wearisome a position as any angler can be placed in; and it would not be strange if, during some moments of this long tussle, he is inclined to the opinion that, after all, it may be true, as the cynic hath said, that angling is an exercise which requires a rod and line with a worm at one end and a fool at the other. But even *such* a struggle has its compensations, and every true angler would gladly bear even tenfold the fatigue involved in such labor rather than surrender one iota of the intensely pleasurable excitement he derives from it. But as there is an end to all things, so there is an end to a salmon's sulks. When well nigh weary to exhaustion, and when almost ready to make the effort to force him from his hole if every inch of rod and tackle should be smashed in the effort, the patient angler found the fish rushing as determinedly as he before had sulked. More than two hundred feet of line went out of the reel in a flash; and it became now even harder to stop than it was before to start him. Rush followed rush in such quick succession that scarcely a yard of line remained in reserve. The only hope was in the equally rapid movement of the canoe. The boatmen were as eager and excited as the fisherman, and whatever muscle could accomplish was done. It was a race for life on one hand and for conquest on the other. In a moment the pool was left far back in the distance. Now one rapid and now another was passed. Shallows were avoided and rocks were shunned with a skill which was as marvelous as the wonderful strength and vitality of the fish. A full mile had been thus gone over with lightning-like velocity. The General had not for a moment lost either his head or his feet. The line was held with an even hand, and the signs indicated a speedy triumph of mind over matter, and skill over brute force, when (may stale fish be his diet for a fortnight!) one of the men, by a wrong movement of his paddle, sent the canoe directly beneath an overhanging tree which compelled the General to lower the tip of his rod, of which the fish took instant advantage, snapped the leader and was off, leaving behind him a cascade of foam and followed by "a blue streak." Such an issue of a hard fight is a terrible test of one's patience, and when his leaderless line came back upon him, limp and empty as a stale joke, if the General had simply said, "Boys, go to camp," he would have proved himself more than mortal. If he uttered any other sentence, the angel's tear which fell upon the hastily spoken word of Uncle Toby, no doubt blotted out all that was superfluous and unseemly.

Other incidents of a like character were constantly occurring. Indeed, the successful capture of a fish that rises to your fly is as frequently the exception as the rule. And this is not to be wondered at when it is remembered that the hook used is not larger than the smallest pin when curved. When the fish rises to this diminutive object, and the angler "strikes," the chances are at least two to one that it will slip out of the huge jaws of the eager fish. And even when the hook catches some part of the exposed surface, it is quite as likely to catch where the fibre is tender as where it is tough. But if hooked just right, there is still the contingency of imperfect tackling, a misshapen hook, a brittle loop, a frayed leader, or a deceptive line; and superadded to all these, are the hidden rocks against which line or leader is often chafed up to the point of separation. With these and many other chances against the angler, the wonder is not that he often loses a fish, but that he succeeds in killing so many. And yet it is this uncertainty — these always possible and frequently occurring contingencies — which give to the science its greatest charm, and make success something of which to be proud.

CHAPTER XI.

SALMON HABITS AND A LOST BATTLE.

A bird in the hand is worth two in the bush.—[*Old adage.*

NOTWITHSTANDING our success, we are every day made conscious that we are too late for the best fishing. Some of the pools from which half a score of salmon could be taken in a day previous to the middle of July, are now barren of fish; and in many others, a day may be consumed in achieving what could then be accomplished in an hour. Salmon begin to run into fresh water early in June, or so soon as the Spring freshets are over; and then they show their greatest life and voracity. From that time on to the middle of July, they are most active and rise most readily to any object which attracts their attention. After that — when they have been a month or more in fresh water — they become somewhat sluggish and less disposed to rise. Besides, the water becomes so shallow and transparent that the very shadow of the line is distinctly visible; and no fish is more shy or more easily frightened. To take a salmon under these circumstances requires the exercise of the greatest patience, and to take them in any great numbers is proof of the very highest skill. I would never advise any one who has to make a long journey to reach salmon waters to go later than the first of July, except on compulsion. Better fish in August than not fish at all, but you will be sure of a larger catch in one week toward the close of June than during a whole month after the fifteenth of July.

It is, however, no proof that there are no salmon in a pool because they do not rise. I have more than once cast all day in a pool alive with leaping salmon — above, below and all around me — without being able to lure one to my hook. This is one of the peculiarities of the fish I cannot fathom. My own experience is the experience of every one who has ever spent even a week upon a salmon river.

It is generally believed that salmon eat nothing after they enter fresh water; and their apparently empty stomachs when dissected are cited in proof of the theory. But if they eat nothing, and have no desire to do so, why do they rise to a living or artificial object? Why do they often even gorge the fly and rise to a minnow, or take a minnow or a fly when trolled under the surface, or when dropped as bait is ordinarily dropped in still fishing? The general absence of food from the stomach is seemingly conclusive of the total abstinence theory; but better believe anything marvelous or improbable than that a salmon lives through six months or any number of months of the year in a state of constant activity, and during the exhaustive process of generation, without imbibing any particle of food. It it just as improbable that it does so as it would be unnatural.

But I have neither the wish nor the knowledge requisite to enter upon an intelligent discussion of any of the habits or peculiarities of this fish. This is neither the purpose nor the intent of these rambling letters.

In my last I referred to some of the more noteworthy incidents which occurred to Gen. ARTHUR. Others had almost equally exciting experiences. None of our party had greater skill, or were made happy by greater success, than Mr. DUN. He kept even pace with the General, and often distanced myself. Of course I attributed this to his longer practice; it could have been nothing else! But while he had his successes he also had his mishaps. The most notable was this: He had hooked a very large fish at the camp-pool, which began the fight magnificently. I never saw a fish leap more spitefully or make more determined efforts to escape. But he was managed so splendidly that at the end of an hour and a half all the lookers-on voted him sure to be bagged. Directly below the pool where he was struck, and to which he had been restricted, was a heavy rapids which the canoe-men were anxious, if possible, to avoid. They advised, therefore, rather than to allow the fish to shoot these rapids, that he should be, as gently as possible, coaxed over to a cove of deep water lying behind some large rocks above the rapids and near the middle of the pool. This advice was taken, and in effecting the change of base the fish gave a series of leaps which revealed the full dimensions of the largest salmon, by many pounds, I ever saw. When asked for an estimate of his weight, the Indian gaffer simply held up his paddle to indicate that that, in his opinion, was about his measure. The desired cove was securely reached. The fish changed his tactics from leaping to sulking, as they most generally do in deep, still water, and at the end of two full hours was seemingly as far from being a dead fish as at any moment during the struggle. Thinking he would be able to manage him better and hold him more comfortably on the rock than in the canoe, Mr. DUN made the transfer, sitting down as coolly and unflurried as if he were casting up the interest on a long note instead of fighting a hard battle with a forty-five-pound salmon. I took my seat beside him, intensely interested in the contest, and endeavored to rest his weary muscles by congratulating him upon the grand sport he was having, and expressing my admiration of the splendid way in which he was handling his fish. But he shook his head doubtfully, and expressed his fears of the issue. "I don't like," he said, "the occasional feel of my line. It seems to me that the fellow is rubbing his nose against a rock, trying to chafe off my leader. There it goes again! I must get out of this or I shall lose him, sure." The fight had been going on now for two hours and fifteen minutes by the watch, and Mr. D. had just made his first step toward the canoe, when up came the broken leader, the sad memento of a lost battle! Just what he feared had happened, and what was undoubtedly the largest fish that had been hooked this season, "turned tail" upon his discomfited captor. And there was silence for the space of a minute. Fisher, gaffer and lookers-on were equally speechless. If any one was tempted to blaspheme, he evidently felt that "he had nothing in his vocabulary at all adequate to the occasion," and said nothing. I had always admired the complacent serenity with which my poor friend had borne the crosses of life, but on this occasion his serenity touched the verge of the sublime. Happy man

TAKING IT EASY.

who can thus lose a (say) fifty-pound salmon without intermitting a single puff of his cigar! Many a saint has been canonized who never exhibited the angelic virtues of uncomplaining submission and gentle patience in such sublime measure.

Another mishap occurred in this wise: When I was fighting what afterward proved to be a thirty-four pound fish (my largest), and just at a most critical moment, I found that my line had become crossed and "doubled under" on my reel. I could take in at pleasure, but I could not let out an inch. It was an awkward fix; but as good luck would have it, by risking an extra strain upon my rod I soon regained more line than was afterward called for, and saved my fish. The dilemma was the result of careless reeling. One cannot be too particular in seeing that his line is reeled up closely and without a lap. I lost a salmon before I thoroughly learned this useful lesson.

These mishaps, however, were but exceptions to the rule of good luck, although it is undoubtedly the experience of most salmon anglers that they miss a great many more fish that rise than they hook, and lose a great many more that are hooked than they kill. At least that was our experience. Enough, however, were killed, and of sufficient weight, to satisfy the ambition of the most ambitious in our party. On the General's large score was marked one fish of forty odd pounds, and several others approximating that weight. Mr. Dun's score fully equaled that of the General, and embraced one or more of the same weight, with several ranging from thirty pounds upward. Col. Pell, with a somewhat smaller score, approached the most successful of the party in weight. My first three fish weighed eighty-eight pounds (30, 24 and 34) and my three largest ninety-three pounds (34, 30 and 29); but my heaviest fish weighed only thirty-four pounds — several pounds less than the largest which honored the scores of Gen. Arthur and Mr. Dun, and less than the largest taken by Col. Pell. In June and early July better scores were made, and a few larger fish were taken — as high as forty-eight pounds — but I am sure no other party was ever better pleased with their achievements or more thoroughly enjoyed the sport.

Our trip to the Forks of the river, nearly fifty miles up stream, with a description of the grand scenery which met us at every step, the beautiful camp we erected and adorned, the grand rapids we ascended, the splendid fishing we had, our return flight through the rapids, with the thousand and one pleasant incidents that made every day too short and the breaking up of camp the only unhappy moment — all these will form the theme of future chapters. I will only now say, in closing this record of my first year's visit to the Cascapedia, that our trip up the river was marked by two unusual occurrences — the sight of a huge Black Bear, which abound in this region, and of a large Moose, which are here as thick as deer in the Adirondacks. The former was "loafing 'round" on a pebbly beach, and the latter was crossing the river, soon after sunrise, in the immediate neighborhood of our camp. All hands were routed out to see him, and the shootist of our party had the good fortune to — *miss him*, although within easy rifle range. But who could hit his first Moose before fairly awake? The monster was as large as a Jersey cow, with great spreading antlers, but he moved as sprightly as a grey-hound when he discovered his proximity to our camp.

It is a pleasure also to say that we remember gratefully the courtesies of Mr. MOFFAT, of Dalhousie, and the unceasing attentions of Mr. MONTGOMERY, Collector of the Port, who made our day's stay in the town one of unalloyed pleasure. Both gentlemen placed our party under lasting obligations, and their kindness and hospitality will always be associated with the pleasant memories we shall ever cherish of our first visit to these salmon waters.

Second Visit to the Cascapedia.

CHAPTER XII.

SOME REMINISCENCES OF OLD FRIENDS.

Did ever any one see the like! What a heap of trumpery is here; and since I find you an honest man, I will make no scruples in laying my treasures before you.—[*Charles Cotton.*

IN taking down my store of angling implements from their winter's repose, I found them as I had left them, after a long siege of service. They were as welcome as the faces of old friends; and the older the more welcome.

There was the identical "silver doctor" with which I took my first salmon last year — dim and frayed from hard service, but more precious from association than all its score of gaudy companions. What any fly would do, under any circumstances, for any one, that fly did for me. Whether in sunshine or cloud — whether in untried waters or where each ripple, rock and eddy were as familiar as household words — whether, when no breeze disturbed the silvery surface of the river or when the storm howled all around me — always and in all places it was true to its office. We sometimes have such friends, and because some such have been brought to mind by this tiny memento of forest life, I will place it on the retired list, lest it should disappoint me should I again test it, and so the pleasant memories I have of it be dimmed by the recollection of a single failure. Even friendship may get weary, and he is wise who never overtasks it.

Here is another memento — a Limerick hook, which proved a faithful friend in all waters for many years. I took my first trout with it in 1853, from a mill-pond not far from Coburg in Canada. The water was as transparent as the atmosphere. I had whipped every inch of it in vain. Not a fish would rise to any fly I could muster. In despair I had resort to bait, and dropping my line into deep water within a few feet of a sunken brush-heap, I was startled on seeing coming out from beneath it, with a sedate and complacent gravity, a massive and graceful trout, evidently quite intent upon the tempting lure which I had placed before him. But he moved very slowly, as if confident that what his eye was fixed upon could not escape him; and as if, like an experienced epicure, he was determined to enjoy in anticipation the feast which he was sure of, he smacked his lips, as trout often do, and dashed at last for the bait. I struck him on the instant, but too soon. I knew he was badly hooked, and felt that to save him would require most careful handling. The bank upon which I stood was three or four feet above the water, and the water two yards from the bank was twenty feet in depth. After a struggle of ten minutes, I saw that with the delicate hold I had of him it would be impossible either to kill or lift him, and having neither landing net nor gaff, JAMES WILD — who as a looker-on was even more excited than myself — begged of me to lead the fish close to the bank, when he could, he thought, by taking the line near the hook, slide him out of the water in safety. I was afraid of the experiment and suggested my hat as a substitute for a landing net; but he, as he always is, was sanguine of success and I submitted. Never was fish led more delicately, and he followed my lead as kindly as a pet lamb, until I held him within three feet of WILD's stand-point. Seizing the line, and poising himself with artistic precision, he slid the beautiful creature out of the water nearly to the top of the bank, when the hook was disengaged, and, with a single shake of his tail, as if in defiance, he plunged back into his native element, and *I after him!* Seeing that the momentum which W. gave him was not sufficient to save him, I instinctively threw myself forward to scoop him up, but failed, and found myself the next instant *coming up* myself through the pure water into which I had plunged in my fruitless efforts to save the fish! WILD never moved a muscle, but pointing to a spot a few rods distant, quietly suggested to me to "swim yonder; it's a good place to get out at!" He has never offered to land a fish for me from that day to this.

I have other pleasant recollections of this Limerick. Trees have been climbed, brooks have been forded, and stout garments have been cut, to preserve it; and here it is to-day, good as new and ready for instant service. I shall preserve it as an heir-loom, and it shall go down to posterity with my "silver doctor" certified, under my hand and seal, as a friend who never failed me.

And here is a Reel, with every movement out of gear and quite as unfit for service as a broken rod. And yet I would as soon think of burning the letters of an old friend as to throw it away; for I never look at it without having come up before me a thousand pleasant reminiscences of angling waters in the Canadas, in Wisconsin, Vermont, New Hampshire, Maine, and the lakes and rivers which make an angler's paradise of our own northern forests. It rendered its first service in the waters of the Chateaugay lakes — once famous as the best trout waters on our northern border. This was so long since that it is like sprinkling snow-flakes upon my frosted locks to think of it. My companions were James Cook, Alfred Clark and Duncan Pell. They have all crossed the dark river; but the recollection of their virtues and good fellowship remains as a pleasant memory. During that excursion I remember that Gen. Cook wagered Mr. Pell that a three-pound-and-a-quarter brook trout I had taken in the inlet could not be beaten. As Mr. Pell had just captured one which weighed five pounds and a quarter, of course the General lost the wager. Both fish, within twenty-four hours, were served up as the crowning dish of a sumptuous dinner given to a select party of friends by Hamilton Fish, then the chief executive of the State as he is now the honored head of the Washington cabinet. It is rare indeed that two such brook trout are ever taken from any of the rivers in our own State. They are common in the Rangely waters, but nowhere else within our own territory this side the Rocky Mountains.

And this "leader" has its history. I bought it in Montreal, years ago, when I found myself too late for a pleasure trip to the Saguenay for salmon. Falling in with an expert, he proposed that we should try the streams intersecting the railroad between Montreal and Portland. The suggestion was an agreeable one, and we were soon pushing our way from Island Pond to a famous brook and lake some five miles distant. The day was intensely hot, and we despaired of success unless we should have the luck to strike a "spring-hole." This, after hours of seeking, we failed to find in the brook; and the lake (whose shores were composed of mud and quick-sand) gave no better promise. But as the sun-glare began to pass from the face of the water, trout were observed to "break" in a narrow circle a few rods distant. There was the "spring-hole" we were seeking. But how to reach it! A log-raft was speedily extemporised, and we had our reward. My "leader" was strung with five flies, and in six casts I killed eighteen trout, weighing nineteen pounds and a half. At one throw I took three which aggregated five pounds and a half. I preserve it as a memento of a happy day.

With this "brown hackle," without intermission, I killed one hundred and nine small trout in four hours in a pond near Racquette Falls. I handle it as gently as a relic, not alone because it is the memento of an unusual achievement, but because the sight of it brings up vividly before me the beautiful lake where the trout lay; its crystal waters; the glinting of its ruffled surface as the bright sun fell upon it; the densely-wooded hills which encircled it; the soughing of the tall pines as the summer's breeze swept through their branches; the deer which, unconscious and unharmed, alternately disported himself upon the sand-beach and fed upon the water lilies whose snowy crests kept time to the music of the gentle waves which rolled up, like long belts of silver, upon the golden sands; and the thrill which coursed through every nerve as trout after trout leaped to the cast, and, after such manipulation and "play" as only those who have had personal experience can comprehend, were duly captured.

And here are discarded lines, unused gimp, broken snells, severed tips, sinkers, floats, trolling gangs, minnow lines, wires, pincers, feathers from duck, peacock and pigeon, wax, thread, loose hooks, spoons and whatever else goes to make up an ancient angler's "kit." They have each filled up the measure of their office, and deserve the repose which they have earned from long use and faithful service.

CHAPTER XIII.

BRIEF TRIBUTE TO A DEPARTED FRIEND.

To die is landing on some silent shore,
Where billows never break, nor tempests roar;
Ere well we feel the friendly stroke, t'is o'er.
— [*Garth.*

Nor kings nor nations
One moment can retard th' appointed hour.
— [*Dryden.*

The world's an inn, and death's the journey's end.
— [*Ibid*

Since then our Arcite is with honor dead,
Why should we mourn that he so soon is freed?
— [*Ibid.*

THE pleasurable emotions usually excited by needed work preparatory to our annual excursion, were chastened upon this occasion by the recollection that one of the four who made up our party last year — the youngest, the most buoyant and the best beloved — will never again join us in our pleasant angling expeditions. Soon after his return home last summer, without premonition, "in the twinkling of an eye," he was called to pass the dark river. His sudden death, from an organic malady which no care could avert, made a happy home desolate, and cast a shadow over many loving hearts. No one of us anticipated a return to the Cascapedia more confidently or with greater delight. But it was not to be. We shall miss him, for he was the life and inspiration of the camp, as he was the ever-welcome guest of every social circle. There only remains to us the recollection of his pleasant ways and joyous companionship.

After his return home, and a few days before his death, he gave expression to the memories he cherished of the Cascapedia in the following beautiful lines:

THE CHALEUR BAY — 1874.

AFTER FATHER PROUT'S SHANDON BELLS.

With deep affection,
And recollection,
I often think of the Chaleur Bay;
Whose river wild, would,
In age or childhood,
Cast round men's fancies, its magic sway.

There memory drifting —
The past uplifting,
Brings well-remembered scenes of summer time;
The sportsman's pleasure,
Or grateful leisure,
On Cascapedia's pine-clad banks sublime.

I've seen the river,
That thundering ever,
Roars at Niagara its mighty tone,
But the bosom smiling,
All care beguiling,
Fair Cascapedia! 'tis all thy own.

The Hudson splendid,
With floods descended
From tow'ring summits, rising range on range.
With stately motion
Moves toward the ocean,
But equals not thy ever beauteous change.

When old and hoary,
From life's dull story
We turn and gaze along our backward way.
Dim eyes will lighten,
And old hearts will brighten,
To see our river on the Chaleur Bay.

—[*D. Archie Pell.*

CHAPTER XIV.

SECOND VISIT TO THE CASCAPEDIA — WHO MADE UP THE PARTY.

Let us to the ancient woods: I say, let us value the woods. They are full of solicitations.—[*Thoreau.*

I leave the town with its hundred noises,
Its clatter and whir of wheel and steam,
For woodland quiet and silvery voices,
With a forest camp by a crystal stream.
—[*G. W. Nears.*

HERE are scores of salmon rivers between Quebec and Labrador, but they are not all equally attractive. In some there are but few fish; in others the fish are uniformly small; in others still there are ten grisle to one salmon; in still others the pools are separated by great distances, and many of them are subject to such sudden floods and such frequent discoloration of their waters as to render fishing precarious and unsatisfactory, except at such remote and uncertain intervals as to weary the most patient angler. There are, however, a multitude of rivers in which the fish are large and abundant.

where the pools are numerous and accessible, where grisle are seldom encountered, and where the scenery is as magnificent as the fishing is superb. A few of these rivers are within easy reach of steamboat, railroad and telegraph communication. Others (and many of the best of them) are so far from these conveniences that business men, who do not care to put themselves wholly beyond the reach of their correspondents, seldom visit them.

Several of both these classes of rivers were available to our party the present season, and it was not until late in May that it was finally determined to revisit the Cascapedia — the scene of our last year's exploits, and, taking it all in all, one of the very best rivers on the continent. While it is as true of angling as of every thing else, that "variety's the very spice of life," we were all glad when this conclusion was reached ; for we had such pleasant recollections of this river — of its grand pools, its monster salmon and its magnificent scenery — that the thought of change was never agreeable.

We proceeded to our destination over the same route as last year — viâ Boston, Portland, Bangor, St. John and Shediac by rail, and thence some three hundred miles by steamboat. The route is a very pleasant one, but neither shorter nor pleasanter than by way of Quebec, from whence a fine steamer leaves once a week, for Gaspe, Dalhousie, Pictou, etc. The sail by this latter route through the Gulf and Bays which intervene, is one of the most delightful imaginable if the weather is pleasant and no fogs show themselves. Those who want to know all about it are referred to Harper's recently published "Guide to the Maritime Provinces."

Dalhousie, where we left the steamer, is "beautiful for situation," but only interesting to anglers as being the centre of several of the best salmon rivers on the continent. The Restigouche empties into the bay of Chaleur in its immediate neighborhood, and the Cascapedia lies on the opposite shore only a few miles distant. The former is by far the larger river, and has abundant room for a score of rods; but while the Cascapedia is of less volume, it is generally preferred, not only because the fish are uniformly larger, but because the pools are more distinctly marked and the scenery more attractive.

And this latter consideration never fails to enter into the calculations of the true angler; for it is a great mistake to assume that his fondness for the art has no other or higher inspiration than the anticipated excitement of catching fish. Many excellent trout streams wend their way, for long distances, through flat lands and tangled morasses.

I have been beguiled to such sluggish streams by glowing representations of large fish and plenty of them. But I could never be tempted to repeat my visit. Half the pleasure, and more, of camp-life depends upon where you pitch your tent. Whoever has imbibed the gentle and poetic spirit of the old masters must have pleasant surroundings or he soon wearies of the sport. To enjoy the pastime in full measure there must be rapid and cascade, rock and mountain, forest and flower, songbird and murmuring waters. The rise and strike and play of a mammoth trout or salmon is to the angler what the stir and bustle and push of commerce is to the man of business. They give buoyancy to the spirits, elasticity to the step, activity to the brain and a quicker flow to the life-currents of the whole system. But this season of busy activity finds delightful relief in the quiet repose of a pleasant home. The tug and swirl and lusty play of a twenty-pound salmon thrills the nerves like an electric current, makes every muscle tingle with ecstacy, and sends the blood coursing through the body as if each particular vein was the highway of an aurora borealis. But even in the midst of the fierce struggle, his eye takes in the scenic beauties with which he is encompassed. He sees the deep pool encircled by the white foam of the swift moving waters; the ponderous bowlders which rise like water-giants all around him; the foaming rapid whose approach is smooth as glass and which reflects back the sun's rays like a polished mirror; the luxuriant foliage which fringes the stream and which is re-produced in even richer hues by the transparent water into which it casts its refreshing shadows; and the cloud-capped hills which are around him "as the mountains are round about Jerusalem."

Of course, the supreme business of the hour when hooked to a fish is to land him, but even this highest source of the angler's pleasure would soon lose its charm, if, during the progress of the struggle, the eye was not occasionally relieved by these visions of beauty. No, it is not all of fishing to fish. If it were, the angler would not be able to claim fellowship with the long line of poets, philosophers, divines and statesmen whose names, from the time of St. Peter to the present hour, have adorned its annals.

Our party consisted of Gen. ARTHUR, R. G. DUN, Judge FULLERTON and myself — the Judge taking the place of our lamented friend PELL, who was called to his rest soon after his return home last August. While we greatly missed him, no more agreeable companion than Judge FULLERTON ever cast a fly or enlivened a camp-fire. He had just escaped from the Brooklyn court-room, where for months he had attracted the attention of the whole country by his masterly examination and cross-examination of witnesses in the famous Beecher trial. The excessive mental labor was most exhausting, and no man anywhere more needed or more deserved the relaxation which nothing so well as angling affords. He had, withal, on the very eve of his departure, met with an accident which compelled the use of a crutch, and which, for a time, threatened to deprive him of the pleasure of the trip and his friends the pleasure of his companionship. But, fortunately, he was able to start, whereat he rejoiced more than when all men praised him for his marvellous professional skill and genius.

Gen. ARTHUR was also an invalid. In spite of his magnificent *physique,* sustained by a constitution perfected by the accumulated vigor of many generations, he had reached the verge of complete exhaustion by overwork and anxiety in the discharge of his onerous and complicated official duties. His great debility resulted in what very soon proved to be a most malignant carbuncle, causing him great suffering and his friends extreme uneasiness. But while his physicians doubted the propriety of his entering upon his purposed journey, he preferred rather to take the risk than to forego the anticipated pleasure. So, with face poulticed and bandaged as if he had been participating in the rough amusements proverbially inseparable from a "Donnybrook Fair," he took his departure full of hope that his ailment would be but temporary, and that he would find on the "fair Cascapedia" that health and vigor of which he had been despoiled in the great metropolis. When, with a few friends, he joined Judge FULLERTON with his crutch, at the pre-arranged rendezvous, they were both subjected to a deal of chaffing, as fitter subjects for a hospital than for a camp-fire, and better representatives of the invalid corps than of the jolly guild of anglers. The Judge, though quite unfitted to lead in a German, had the free use of his tongue and paid the gibers back in their own coin; but the General was muzzled. He could only look his pity that gentlemen so sensible in all else so little appreciated the pleasure which awaited him, as to assume that anything short of a positive providential prohibition could prevent any one who had ever experienced the supreme delectation of angling, from carrying out his purpose to "go a-fishing." But the exhibition was comical, nevertheless, and the humor of it was quite as fully enjoyed by the invalids as by their friends.

As the sequel proved, it would have been well had the General taken the advice of his physician; for his illness mastered him before he reached his destination. Two weeks of intense suffering was the result. But his purpose remained unchanged; and so soon as he could be safely lifted from his couch he started off to meet us — weak but hopeful — assured that nothing would so soon set him up as the "strike" of a salmon and the joyous *abandon* of camp-life. And he was right. He had been taking his twenty grains of quinine every day for a fortnight. His first salmon made his torpid blood leap with all the vitality of lusty health. He very soon discarded his medicine, as he found every pound of salmon the full equivalent of a grain of quinine. In forty-eight hours he was my chief competitor at table, a fact which enabled the Judge to render the formal decision that he was a well man with a ravenous appetite. For a week the Judge limped his way to his canoe by aid of his crutch; but after that he was our champion pedestrian. There is something magical in the atmosphere of this far-north region, when to its health-giving properties is superadded the excitement afforded by the pleasant pastime of angling.

CHAPTER XV.

IN CAMP — THE INDIAN GAFFER — THE ADVANTAGES OF PRESERVED WATERS.

Here, or in some such devoted solitude, should dwell the Muse and compose a treatise on the worship of the Dryads.—
[*Thoreau.*

Blessed silent groves! O may you be
Forever mirth's best nursery!
     May pure contents
     Forever pitch their tents
Upon these downs, these meeds, these rocks, these mountains,
And peace still slumber by the purling fountains,
    Which we may every year
    Meet, when we come a-fishing here.
               — [*Sir Henry Wotton.*

OUR first camping ground was twelve miles from the mouth of the river and combined all the elements of picturesqueness and grandeur — a verdant plain encircled by lofty mountains, only broken by a cleft of sufficient breadth to give egress to the crystal river, whose leaping waters filled our camp with perpetual melody. We reached it, as last year, by canoes which awaited our coming, and of which we instantly availed ourselves to reach our coveted Mecca. I was greatly pleased to find that my last year's guides were again at my service. I wished no better, and I was flattered by their salutation and their assurance that they wished to render service to no more patient angler. No one of the party had reason to murmur at the men assigned him. All seemed equally expert with paddle and setting pole, and all, with a single exception, could gaff his fish at the right moment and with mathematical precision. If they occasionally missed, and, by a false stroke, lost their prize, it is only what sometimes happens to the best and wisest in every department of life. What a "raree show" for an admiring world would that man be who had never blundered! Of some of the mistakes made in gaffing, and of the effect of these mistakes upon the mild-tempered gentlemen who were the victims of them, I shall have something to say hereafter — only remarking now, in passing, that skill in gaffing is considered the highest accomplishment of an Indian guide. I have seen feats of skill by gaffers which were marvelous in their lightning-like rapidity and magical dexterity. The Indian is at no time so wholly an Indian as when, with flashing eye and distended nostril — with every nerve strung for the work before him, and with attitude as fixed and immovable as a marble statue — he is awaiting his opportunity to gaff his fish. It is the poise of the eagle awaiting the auspicious moment to dash upon his selected victim; the crouching of the lion ready to leap upon his prey. No angler's gallery is perfect without a picture of an Indian gaffer thus ready to strike.

Each canoe has two guides. Both are necessary to propel the frail craft over the impetuous rapids which are met with in every salmon river; and they are equally necessary in guiding the canoe down the rapids, which are generally boiling cauldrons, full of rocks and whirlpools and treacherous currents. Running, as these rapids often do, ten or fifteen miles an hour, contact with a rock is full of peril. But this seldom happens. I remember but a single instance, and that was the result of overloading rather than the lack of skill or judgment in the canoemen.

Two hours of steady pulling brought us to our camp, where we found several fishers who had been awaiting our coming to strike their tents and leave the river. They had had good sport, but not equal to that of last year. Why? was a question they were unable to answer. Most likely because they came too late to meet the first run of fish, which were believed to have passed up at the full of the spring freshet, when successful angling is not deemed practicable, and when even tide-water fishing with nets is seldom attempted. This theory was partially confirmed by the fact that those who had gone to the upper pools had no cause of complaint. Ordinarily, the best time to "whip" a river is when the first spring freshet is subsiding. Then the fish are fresh from the sea and far more eager and muscular than after a long sojourn in fresh water. Except upon compulsion, no one should defer his visit to a salmon river later than the middle of June. On a good river there will be tolerable fishing until the middle of August, but the cream of the sport is only available on this river from the tenth of June to the fourth of July. It was not our luck, either last year or this, to be able to choose our time. We hope, however, to do so on some future occasion. We shall then know whether it is possible to experience any higher pleasure, or to achieve any grander successes, than have rendered memorable our two visits to the Cascapedia.

As is the manner of all true anglers, our unknown friends gave us a most hearty welcome. Their spacious board was loaded with every coveted delicacy, freshly caught and artistically cooked salmon constituting, of course, the chief and most palatable dish. And salmon only reveal their unapproachable delicacy when thus served. If the fastidious *gourmand* is rendered happy by such stale specimens of the delicious fish as he has served up to him a thousand miles from where they are caught, into what spasms of ecstacy would he be thrown by partaking of the delicate morsel while the golden flakes still retain their full and luscious flavor! Such golden flakes melted upon our palates on this pleasant occasion; and if no sparkling wines were brought forward to crown the feast, we found a better substitute in an abundant supply of excellent coffee, far more delicious to our taste than would have been the fabled "nectar of the gods."

After a hasty adieu and a whole volume of good wishes, we were left temporary "monarchs of all we surveyed," and, with two beside — Captain GRANT, of England, and Mr. KINEAR, of St. John — the sole occupants of fifty miles of as splendid salmon waters as ever received the fly of a jolly angler.

Camp-life in pleasant weather on trout stream or salmon river, with agreeable companions and passable sport is, to the angler, the very perfection of enjoyment. He covets nothing so much as these periodical respites from rasping care and social conventionalities. They are full of sunshine in their realization, and they remain a pleasant memory forever.

Our first camping ground was all that heart could wish — a charming valley, encircled by an amphitheatre of mountains, wood-clad to their very summit, with the river, transparent as the atmosphere, moving in graceful undulations to the sea. It took but a few hours to pitch our tents, to extemporise a dining hall and kitchen, and to settle down to the solid comfort and enjoyment coveted by those whose simple tastes lead them to these quiet places.

There are, popularly, erroneous ideas entertained of the comforts or discomforts of camp-life. These ideas have been for the most part derived from the real or imaginary pictures painted by novices in wood-craft. One may be quite as comfortable in a bark or log shanty or under a canvas tent as in a well appointed hostelry. It only requires a knowledge of what is essential to comfort and the experience necessary to apply this knowledge practically. To "rough it" does not necessarily imply wet feet, damp clothing, a hard bed, insufficient covering, a leaky tent, hard tack and stale bacon. These are all available to those who prefer them, and the chances are ten to one that you will have them all until you learn that none of them are either necessary or desirable. If you cannot procure what I have found to be unprocurable (waterproof leather boots), a pair of thick rubber shoes, for wet days and damp places, will keep your feet dry. With a rubber coat and leggings, except in a drenching tempest, you need wear no damp clothing. A piece of heavy canvas, with open seams through which to pass your extemporised stretchers, will give you a spring bed, which, with aromatic balsam boughs for a mattrass and plenty of blankets to keep you warm, makes as comfortable a couch as you can buy of the upholsterer. A leaky tent or shanty is an unnecessary nuisance; while, by using a little forethought, your *cuisine* may be as palatable and healthful as any epicure could desire. It all depends upon one's own skill and knowledge, and these, like all wisdom, are only acquired by experience.

Nor to attain these comforts is it necessary to render yourself ridiculous by transporting a cart-load of luggage. A large sack, which any one can shoulder, will hold your A or wall-tent, your bedding and all your rough garments. A hand valise is sufficient for your "store clothes." Two or three moderate sized packages will cover your necessary provender for an ordinary trip, and your tackling is easily portable. A Saratoga trunk on trout-stream or salmon river is as conclusive as a sonorous bray that a donkey is in the neighborhood. Yet these are sometimes seen, ordinarily accompanied by a biped decked off in long boots, velvet pants and jacket, a jaunty hat bedizzened with gaudy flies, and a body belt ornamented with bowie knife and pistol, as if he expected at every turn to encounter herds of wild cats or panthers, or a whole tribe of blood-thirsty Indians anxious for his precious scalp. All anglers in their wanderings have encountered such comical specimens of cockney sportsmen. They are generally harmless, however, catching but few fish and killing too little game to materially affect the supply.

It is the attractive feature of these preserved waters that they can only be fished by those holding official permits to do so. In starting for a pool, your anticipations of sport are not disturbed by the apprehension that it may have already been seized and held by some "earlier bird" than yourself. It is all your own, to make the most of how and when you please. This conscious security comports with the leisurely habits of the true angler, and prevents those feelings of envy, strife and jealousy which are too often excited when one finds a favorite bit of water swept by a bevy of bait-fishers and lashed into foam by their whip-cord lines and heavy sinkers swung out from "larraping rods" huge enough to lift a leviathan. Here you pay for what you have, and you are sure to have what you pay for. No sly departures! No lying awake all night to "steal the march" of your neighbors in the morning! No studied deception! No unseemly racing to get ahead of "the other fellows!" Your assigned pool waits for you, whether the fish do or not; and you cast without haste or fear of disturbance, as the honored guest takes his ease in his inn. How many weary miles I have paddled and tramped among the Adirondacks to get out of the reach of the huge army of "Murray's fools," who for a time swarmed that angler's paradise, with no more appreciation of the art, or of the delectable recreation of angling than a donkey has of the heavenly harmonies. I owe to them, however, the pleasant recollection of many weeks of delightful solitude and repose amid pathless woods and unfrequented lakes and streamlets. So I forgive them — glad, nevertheless, to be able, here, upon the far-off Cascapedia, to fish undisturbed, and to feast upon the magnificent scenery which everywhere meets the eye and gladdens the spirit, without fear of molestation from cockney intruders. This assured isolation during the hours set apart for angling constitutes one of the chief charms of these preserved waters. "Yet" (as that most lovable lover of nature, Thoreau, says) "I would not insist upon any one's trying it who has not a pretty good supply of internal sunshine; otherwise he would have, I judge, to spend too much of his time in fighting with his dark humors. To live alone comfortably, we must have that self-comfort which rays out of nature — a portion of it at least."

Forest solitudes, away off upon and beyond the verge of civilization, have an irresistible fascination. To be alone becomes a passion with some men. There are to-day, as there have been in all the past, hundreds of hunters and trappers in the wilderness of the far west who cannot endure contact with their fellow men, and are only happy when remote from all human habitations. But this exaggerated love of isolation — of perpetual separation from their kind — is no proof of intellectual superiority or of an exalted appreciation of the beauty and grandeur of nature uncontaminated by the depravities and meannesses of a selfish civilization. Moral or esthetic considerations seldom enter the minds of these "mighty hunters." Their hermit-life is simply proof of a morbid and distorted condition of mind, which is neither to be commended, admired nor imitated. It would be as untruthful and as unjust to associate the angler who seeks, temporarily, for repose and recreation, the solitudes of the forest, with these uncouth, unkempt and unlettered trappers, as it would be to proclaim all angling debasing because professional "pot-hunters," who are alike indifferent to times and seasons and the processes by which they achieve results, engage in it.

Nor must it be inferred that isolation is the fixed status of the angler. At proper times and seasons in no class of men is the social element more fully developed. To have this demonstrated it is only necessary to visit the camp-fire after the sports of the day are over. John Wilson's "*Noctes Ambrosiana*" and "*Dies Borealis*," are no mere fictions. His unapproachable dialogues have their counterpart under many another canvas in our own primitive forests. They may not always be marked by the profound philosophy, rollicking humor, tender pathos, or glowing imagery which have given the recorded sayings of these eminent anglers a foremost place among the classics of the century. But they are kindred in tone and spirit, and often approach them in all the good qualities which will render them the delight of all thoughtful men of all the ages.

It is the recollection of these social re-unions, participated in by men of kindred tastes and sympathies, who have sought these far-off solitudes to be happy in their own simple way, quite as much as the strike and struggle of the gamey salmon, which makes the memory of these seasons of recreation and repose "a joy forever." Those who do not find it so have not yet imbibed the spirit of the Fathers, nor attained unto the highest possibilities of the gentle art.

CHAPTER XVI.

A PLEASANT MORNING—THE JUDGE'S FIRST SALMON.

'Neath cloistered boughs each floral bell that swingeth,
   And tolls its perfume on the passing air,
Makes Sabbath in the field, and ever ringeth
      A call to prayer.
            —[*Horace Smith.*

Give me mine angle. We'll to the river; there,
My music playing afar off, I will betray
Tawny finn'd fishes; my bended hook shall pierce
Their slimy jaws; and as I draw them up,
I'll think them every one an Antony,
And say, "Ah, ha! you're caught."
            —[*Shakspeare.*

OUR first morning in camp was cloudless and serene. The "callar mountain air" was pure and bracing. The gentle western breeze came down from the hills freighted with the perfume of a million flowers and the melody of a thousand songsters, calling up the beautiful apostrophe of the psalmist: "Praise waiteth for Thee, O God, in Zion; I will lift up mine eyes unto the hills from whence cometh my help; my help cometh from the Lord, which made heaven and earth." The leaves, besprinkled with "the dew of the morning," sparkled like diamonds in the sunlight, while the river murmured out its perpetual anthem as it moved along its cleft pathway to the sea. Here and there, on the high-up summits of the hills which encircled the beautiful valley in which we had pitched our tents, the morning mist, transparent as a bridal veil, hung in mid-air like a benediction, while every forest tree and flowering shrub swayed to and fro like a waving censer before the grand altar of nature.

And in due time, as if to fill up the measure of our devout gratitude to a kind Providence for having permitted us to "cast our lines in such pleasant places," there came up from the camp-fire the odor of broiled salmon, mingled with the aroma of slowly distilling Mocha, whetting the already keen appetite for the morning meal in rapid preparation. And when served, "there was silence for the space of half an hour," when the Judge held up his crutch in speechless thanksgiving for such a luscious repast amid such gorgeous surroundings.

The first business in order was the allotment of pools. There are three within easy distance of the camp. Each usually affords ample sport, but one of them is more coveted than the others because it uniformly abounds in larger fish. As the Judge had never taken a salmon, this pool was awarded him by unanimous assent—a striking illustration of the self-sacrificing courtesy which distinguishes all true disciples of the gentle art. For, be it understood, it is no mean proof of magnanimity to voluntarily surrender to another the best place to fish. It requires more grace than to give up a "sure thing" in Wall street. This latter sacrifice goes no deeper than the pocket; the former touches the core of your highest enjoyment. Whoever makes this sacrifice has the spirit of the good Samaritan. All anglers may not be thus magnanimous, and those who are do not always find their magnanimity appreciated. But such is the experience of all doers of good deeds. Charitable men, and men of kindly sympathies, are as often accused of ostentation as commended for benevolence. No matter if they do try to "do good by stealth and blush to find it fame," there are critics who will pronounce their modesty hypocrisy, and their blushes the flush of anger that their charities are not proclaimed from the house-top. Not so the Judge. He appreciated the well-meant compliment, and gave due expression to the feeling of gratitude which this "offering of friendship" excited in his "manly bosom."

The issue of this little bit of courtesy was much more satisfactory than a similar instance of piscatorial self-sacrifice which I remember. It occurred in the "North Woods," on one of the inlets which connect the Fulton chain of lakes. I was having excellent sport; almost every cast met with a response, and my creel was becoming unpleasantly weighty with its precious burden. Just as I had reached the margin of a favorite pool from which I had never failed to beguile a half dozen large fish, I observed in the near distance a clever fellow who was passionately fond of the sport, but who, having no skill, had no "luck." "I don't understand it," was his stereotyped bewailment. And just here was his trouble; he did *not* "understand it." He persisted in whipping the stream with a line of four-fold the proper dimensions, and made his casts with a rod equally out of proportion. I, however, liked his pluck and patience, and seeing my opportunity to do him a favor, I invited him to take my place at the pool into which I was about to cast. Although this happened twenty years ago I have not to this day been quite able to decide whether (remembering the sequel) I did a generous or a foolish thing in thus surrendering my prerogative to one who, however grateful, proved himself illy qualified to make the best possible use of his opportunity. His huge sinker fell into the water with a splash, carrying with it a number-nine hook covered with a full half ounce of wriggling worms, when it was at once seized by a three-pound trout, which in another instant was dangling from the limb of a neighboring tree into which he had been elevated by the excited angler. And there he hung for twenty minutes from an inextricably tangled line, which was only recovered, with what depended from it, after such turbulence as to render any further angling in that pool impracticable for the day. But in spite of his awkwardness he saved his trout, was made happy by his success, and overwhelmed me with thanks for my courtesy.

The Judge may not have been more grateful, but he entered upon his work with more grace and skill. His first casts were made with becoming caution, as if feeling his way for the open joints in the harness of a crafty witness. He was too wise an angler to drop his fly into the centre of the pool abruptly. Like a wary General, he worked his way to the heart of the citadel by "gradual approaches." A novice would have charged him with undue timidity, just as impatient lookers on sometimes accused him of irrelevancy when cautiously drawing the net of his irresistible logic around his bewildered victim in the witness box during that famous Brooklyn combat of intellectual giants. He knew what he was about then; he knows what he is about now. He was too wise a lawyer to thwart himself by inordinate haste; and he is too skillful an angler to hazard success by undue precipitancy. Foot by foot his casts were lengthened and swept gracefully across the current of the pool. Foot by foot he worked his way to the objective point, where rested what he coveted more than the verdict of judge or jury. And now, at last, the fly drops gently upon the glistening surface of the dark water, just at the point desired, when there followed a rush and strike, and a momentary pause, as if fish and fisher were alike astounded, and then click, whiz, whir-r-r went the reel, as if harnessed to a lightning train with a thunderbolt for a locomotive. Away went the fish with two hundred feet of line, but stopping at that distance as suddenly as if arrested by a peremptory order of the court. Then came the tug of war; first to hold him — that required muscle; then to bear with him while he sulked — that required patience. The Judge had both, and both were brought into skilful requisition. For ten minutes not a fin stirred; but the taut line, as it resisted the combined pressure of the current and the fish, thrummed like an æolian harp, and made every nerve tingle with delight. As became the watchful angler that he is, the eyes of the Judge were immovably fixed upon his line as it stretched out straight before him. He believed the fish near the opposite bank in a direct line with his rod, and he was looking intently for some sign of life from the spot where he supposed his fish was sulking, when click! click! whiz-z-z, again went the reel, and a huge fish leaped his whole length out of water a hundred feet *above* him. "Hello," said the Judge, "there's another fellow!" "No, that's your fish," said the Indian gaffer. "Blazes! you don't say? What's he doing there? He's not within a hundred feet of my line." "It's your fish, sir. The swift current makes your line bend like the new moon." And this was the fact; but the illusion was so perfect that it required several like experiences to convince him that his Indian gaffer was not "fooling him" upon that occasion.

After an hour's struggle, and with a skill and judgment which excited the admiration of all who witnessed the contest, the fish was killed and captured. When he kicked the beam at the twenty eight pound notch, the Judge was a proud and a happy man. There are many things he will forget as old Time weaves silver threads amid his auburn locks, but he will never forget his astonishment when that fish showed himself one hundred feet from the point where he was intently watching him.

The next day Dun was awarded the Judge's pool and had his usual luck — making a larger score than any of us, and breaking more rods; not because he had less general skill, but because he

THE JUDGE ASTONISHED.

could not receive a challenge from a fish without returning an impetuous "strike" on the instant. One may "strike" too soon as well as too late. In angling, as in everything else, there is a "happy mean"— just the right mode and moment to strike your fish without imperilling your tackling or tearing the hook from his mouth. To invariably compass this right moment requires steadier nerve, greater forbearance and a nicer appreciation of time and opportunity than falls to the lot of most anglers. A few have the gift; but it only comes to old trout fishers after much practice and many discomfitures.

Our friend had been casting half an hour at "a gay gambolier" whose special vocation seemed to be to leap at nothing and keep just a tail's breadth from the lure sent to him. His disportings proved his agility but were provokingly tantalizing; and DUN was just ready to give him up as "a hopeless case," when he made a dash for the fly and was astonished to find himself hooked. With a rush and a leap which eclipsed all his previous demonstrations, he started for the opposite shore as if in a hurry to deliver some message he had forgotten. It was just the last place in the neighborhood of the pool one cared to have his fish take to, for it was full of jagged rocks and hidden bowlders. Aware of this, DUN instantly did his best to bring him back into open water. But after a few desperate tugs, he was compelled, for the time, to give up the effort and permit him to sulk — preserving, however, a taut line, measured with mathematical nicety, upon the stubborn brute. Salmon will sometimes sulk thus for hours, in seeming disregard and contempt of any pressure you dare bring upon them. For more than thirty minutes DUN sat

"Like Patience on a monument, smiling at Grief,"

when he deemed it high time to assume the aggressive. So he ordered his canoemen to paddle cautiously toward the "objective point," while he reeled up his two hundred feet of taut line until every muscle ached with the pressure. He had reached within fifty feet of his leader, but not a tail wagged; thirty feet, but nothing was felt but the steady tension of the quivering line; ten feet, the same. All was as still and motionless as the old granite bowlder which looked down upon the dark waters amid whose eddying currents leader and fly were hidden from vision. Angler and gaffer were alike perplexed. So near a fish and no sign of life! Nothing like it had passed into the annals of angling. "Slide your paddle down cautiously and start him," said DUN. Down slid the paddle, but nothing came of it. "Try again; but take care that he doesn't rush under the canoe."

Down again went the paddle, when, mystery of mysteries! it struck, not a salmon, but the rock around which the salmon had twisted the leader, broken loose from the fly and so escaped, a wiser if not a better fish, quite prepared to resume his game of leap-frog long before his disappointed captor could reel in *the fifty ton bowlder at which he had been tugging lustily for more than thirty minutes!*

Our conversation in camp was of rather a frivolous character that evening. We were afraid to introduce any *weighty* subject lest our friend should interpret it as a personal reflection!

CHAPTER XVII.

DIFFERENCE IN FISH — GAFFING SALMON — THE REEL-CLICK.

Doubt not, sir, but that Angling is an art, and an art worth your learning : the question is, rather, whether you be capable of learning it.—[*Sir Izaak Walton.*

IN one sense, all salmon, like all men, are alike : but like all men, also, they are very unlike in behavior under given circumstances. I once brought a fifteen-pound salmon to gaff in ten minutes, and I have had a two hours' struggle with others of no greater weight; just as some men succumb when so much as a shadow of adversity crosses their pathway, while others fight on so long as a peg remains to hang a hope upon. The former are the negatives of the race, only useful in swelling the numerals of a census table. The latter not only "conquer fate" by their pluck and energy, but are the architects of towns, cities, states and empires. It is only when "Greek meets Greek" that there "comes the tug of war," and it is only when the angler strikes a fighting salmon that he properly appreciates their muscular energy and great endurance.

It is not always possible to give a reason for the difference in the play of different fish of the same species. Every one has his theory. One says it is in the sex. Another, that it depends upon their recent or remote advent into fresh water, and others upon where the fish is hooked. It is undoubtedly true that, as a rule, there is more game in the male than in the female salmon, and that fish fresh from the ocean are the most muscular and ferocious. But I have had equal sport with fish of either sex, and have found as tough customers fifty miles from the sea as in close proximity to it. The difference, I fancy, depends upon how and where they are hooked. A barb through the tongue of a salmon is like a curb on the jaws of a horse; he may have the disposition to run, but he doesn't fancy the unpleasant sensation which follows his attempt to do so. Another reason is, the seeming dull perception of some fish. Like some men, it takes them a good while to get over their astonishment at finding something wrong, and before they really comprehend the situation, they lose their advantage and are gaffed.

I had a very interesting illustration of this one day. I was fishing at a point where counter currents met, and where, consequently, it was difficult to keep out a straight line without constant casting. Becoming weary with this sort of perpetual motion, I allowed my line to slacken and my fly to perambulate at its own sweet will. While they were thus floating in a circle, the fly out of sight, I felt a slight tug and began to reel up leisurely, annoyed that my lure had, as I supposed, been taken by a trout. Every movement, for half a minute, seemed to confirm this impression, and I had stopped reeling to give expression to my disappointment, when the fish started in gallant salmon style, leaped his full length out of water, and gave me all I could do for three hours and twenty minutes before he was brought to gaff, and then he was only struck by a chance blow as he was rushing, in full life, past my canoe in swift water. What I supposed, at first, to be merely a two or three-pound trout proved to be a twenty-seven-pound salmon. If I had been in shoal water when I first reeled him up to within twenty feet of my canoe, I might have ended his career in ten minutes. The hook had struck him at some callous point, and he followed the gentle lead I gave him without sense of pain or danger, and only made a dash when he saw the canoe with its threatening surroundings.

In gaffing this fish while on the run in swift water, my Indian guide proved himself an expert in the most difficult department of the art. The expression of my surprise and admiration made him a happy Indian. He knew he had done something which deserved commendation, and it pleased him to find that it was observed. In our every day life we are too sparing of our compliments. When any one within the circle of our acquaintance does well — whether hod-carrier or Senator, crossing-sweeper or orator — it does no harm to let him know that his well-doing is recognized and appreciated. Judicious commendation is a more potent stimulant than we are apt to think. But for it, many who have come to excel in their several vocations would have grown up into the merest mediocrity, while for lack of it, multitudes have ceased to struggle, because they have received no token that their aspirations were approved. A good word, where deserved, costs nothing, but it is often magical in its effects. My simple " Bravo! no Indian on the Cascapedia could have done better," was more to my guide than are the plaudits of the multitude to the orator on the rostrum. I never afterward lost a fish from want of diligence on the part of my gaffer.

But others did. Dun had hooked a very large fish and had fought him bravely for two hours — bringing him frequently within the reach of his gaffer, and as frequently was obliged to give him line to prevent him from breaking off in his fright when foully struck at. Finally the gaffer reached him, struck out wildly, scratched the fish and snapped the leader! The silence which followed was a grand exhibition of fortitude and forbearance. It may have been that my friend could find no words suitable to the occasion; but I preferred to attribute the Christian-like grace with which he succumbed to the inevitable, to the possession of that rare virtue commended by the Scripture: "Greater is he that ruleth his spirit than he that taketh a city." That gaffer gaffed no more for DUN.

A like misfortune happened to General ARTHUR not long afterward, under even more provoking circumstances. He had hooked his fish, played him with consummate skill and brought him several times to the very feet of his gaffer — the last time seemingly a dead fish and into water not twelve inches deep. But a spell seemed to be on the poor Indian. He struck once, twice, thrice, without effect — except upon the leader, which he broke. But even then the fish did not stir, neither did the gaffer. The fish seemed bewildered, as the gaffer certainly was, until the General quietly intimated that as the fish was waiting to be gaffed it would be well to gratify him; when the Indian seemed to comprehend the situation, and proceeded to do what, if he had attempted two seconds sooner, would have been a success. But before the gaff fell where the fish was he wasn't there, and thirty-five pounds of as fine salmon as ever wagged a tail floated off with the current, in all probability to die "unwept, unhonored and unsung." Expletives, like notes in music, are modulated to meet the intensity of the emotions. The General's expletive was pitched on the upper register, and the gaffer would have been pitched into the Cascapedia if he hadn't looked as if that was just what he expected. The explanation was that the water was not deep enough to permit the gaff-hook to go under the fish. The consequence was it glanced along its side and back, struck the leader, which it broke, and gave the fish free rein. And yet this mishap occurred to one of the most skillful and careful gaffers on the river. The poor fellow hung his head for a week, but it was the last fish he lost.

If it requires skill to always gaff a fish, it requires equal skill to always properly respond to a fish which leaps while the angler is playing him. To elevate your rod as the fish leaps, and to hold it at the attained elevation as he goes down, is to almost inevitably lose him. All that is necessary to be done at this supremely exciting moment, is to let the tip of the rod descend with the fish.

You thus prevent the strain and snap which must otherwise ensue. This movement of the rod at the right instant, under such circumstances, is the most difficult lesson to learn in the whole art of angling. No incident in the sport is more exciting than these salmon leaps. If you do not then preserve your wits you will most certainly lose your salmon. The lesson I learned in maple pool (of which anon) in this direction, was a lesson which I had to learn sooner or later; but the recollection of it will be a grief forever.

What the long-roll is to the soldier the reel-click is to the angler. It is the call to battle and stirs the blood like the sound of a trumpet.

No salmon ever takes the hook when alarmed. He may come to it with a rush, but with his motion so exactly graduated as to have but little momentum after the lure is reached — like a jumper making for the goal. The result is that on the very instant of striking the reel seldom gives out more than a click or two, unless the angler strikes simultaneously — which most anglers do; whether wisely or not, is a problem yet unsolved by the masters of the art. The moment, however, the fish feels the sting of the hook he shoots off with a rush, causing, by his rapid movement, that whiz and whir-r which, to the angler, is the most thrilling music that ever falls upon his ear. The deliberate click, click, which succeeds the strike, is the measured prelude to the grand chorus which follows when the astonished fish enters upon his mad career. These sounds alternate through the protracted struggle; now a single click, as the fish shakes his head in his sulking moments, and now a whiz and whir-r-r, as he rushes and leaps in his desperate efforts to free himself from the stinging barb which holds him. When a determined fish is thus hooked, the same stirring music is repeated a hundred times, until, finally, the poor fellow is only able to give spasmodic tugs, moving the line but the length of a single cog, the reel responding by slow and measured clicks like the tap of a muffled drum beating

"Funeral marches to the grave."

But these death-tugs are full of peril. More fish "tear out" then than at any other moment of the struggle. To prevent such a catastrophe requires the most watchful and delicate manipulation. Safety lies in a cautious easing off of the pressure on the line with every movement of the fish, being careful, however, that no slack is allowed to render his vicious wrench effective and fatal. To see an angler at the moment when a mammoth salmon thus escapes — his rod at the perpendicular, his line dangling loosely in the breeze, his mouth wide open, and his muscles limp as a seaweed — is to see a comical embodiment of disgust, astonishment and despair. His bewailment and self-upbraidings find expression in the unspoken thought: "With a little more care how different 'it might have been.'" All salmon fishers have passed through this experience and understand it. No others can, however graphically described. Did not the poet have this picture in his mind when he wrote:

> Then she took up her burden of life again,
> Saying only: "It might have been."
> God pity them both and pity us all
> Who vainly the dreams of our youth recall;
> For of all the sad words of tongue or pen,
> The saddest are these: "It might have been."

There is but one sound in nature, animate or inanimate, which at all resembles the whir of a reel when in full play — the rattling trill of a kingfisher when on the wing. It is a singular coincidence that the music of the best angler known to ornithology finds its most perfect counterpart in that which man finds indispensable to *his* successful pursuit of a pastime that constitutes *its* life-long vocation. This bird most abounds on swift-running waters. They are in great numbers on the Cascapedia, and more than once my reel and this feathered angler have joined in a duet, to my great amusement and delight. They were in as perfect accord as if brought into concert pitch by the hand of the same master.

CHAPTER XVIII.

TROUT FISHING — DO FISH HEAR? — A MERRY MAKING.

I love such mirth as does not make friends ashamed to look upon one another next morning.—[*Sir Izaak Walton.*

SALMON fishing is confessedly the highest department in the school of angling. With very rare exceptions, the tact and skill necessary for its successful practice is only acquired by long experience in the minor branches of the art, first, in early youth, with bait, for chub, perch and sunfish; next, in the transition state, with troll, for bass, pickerel and muscalonge; and lastly, when the mind takes in the exciting realities and poetic possibilities of the art, with fly, in streamlet, river and lake. It is not until after all is attained that is attainable in trout waters that salmon are sighed for, and only very few who thus sigh are ever able to have their longings gratified. But those whose experience has been limited to bait or troll seldom aspire to anything beyond the pleasant amusement which these primitive modes of angling afford them. Having never cast a fly they have no conception of the superiority of that mode of angling over all others, and so soon weary of a pastime which, from its sameness and tameness, fails to attract when something more than mere muscular exercise or physical excitement is required to hold its votaries. A gray-haired bait-fisher is very rare, while the passion for fly-casting, whether for trout or salmon, grows by what it feeds upon, and continues a source of the highest pleasure even after the grasshopper becomes a burden. But this is not strange; for there is as much difference between these extremes of the art as there is between the harsh music of a hurdy-gurdy and the divine harmony of the violin.

There is, however, such a similarity between trout and salmon fishing that pleasure can be found in either by the expert in both. And as trout usually abound in salmon waters, they are often fished for as a rest from the heavy work involved in the capture of salmon.

Judge FULLERTON had been familiar with trout streams from his youth up. There are few brooks or rivers where trout "most do congregate," from Maine to New Brunswick, in which he has not "slain his thousands." I was not surprised, therefore, to find him very early hankering after a day's hunt for trout. Nor was I any more surprised to find him returning to camp long before half the day was over, with thirty-five pounds of splendid fish, ranging from half a pound to three pounds in weight. Subsequently he met with even greater success — once taking forty-five pounds during a short afternoon. As an experiment, I myself caught sixteen large trout in thirty minutes, with an eight-ounce rod, without a landing net. It was unsportsmanlike sport. My only excuse was to see what could be done in these waters; and as the fish could all be put to good use, there was no waste and consequently no upbraidings of conscience.

The trout in the Cascapedia, and, indeed, in all these salmon rivers, are mostly sea trout, running up the rivers every season, like salmon, to spawn. When they leave the salt water, their spots have scarcely the slightest tinge of crimson. Later, they assume a somewhat brighter hue; but they never attain the beautiful brilliancy of the brook-trout in our home streams. Nor, as a rule, do they rise as sprightly to the fly. Indeed, like salmon, they usually strike without projecting themselves so much as their head's length above the surface. But they are strong, and as they run much larger than the average brook-trout in any of our home waters (save, perhaps, the Rangely lakes), they afford splendid play, and often draw the angler away from the more kingly but far more laborious sport which salmon afford.

There are in these waters brook as well as sea-trout, but they are found mostly in or near the mouths of the small streams emptying into the main river. When we coveted a meal of them, ranging from two to four ounces, we knew just where to find them, and, what is equally important, just how to *crisp* them. There may be a more delicious dish than small brook-trout properly cooked, just as there may be a more delicious fruit than the strawberry, but the fact has not yet passed into the annals of modern discovery.

It may not be out of place nor uninteresting to some of my readers to say, while I think of it, that I took some pains to gather the opinions of our Indian guides on the mooted question, "Do fish hear?" To my surprise I found that there was but one opinion — the negative of the question. And a great many facts were given in support of this opinion, much to my satisfaction, as I have for a long time been fully satisfied that all fish are "deaf as adders."

This question was amusingly discussed the other day. Having arranged to change camp, we requested one of the baggage canoe-guides, who moved off a day in advance of us, to mark two or three spots which he knew to be good casting places, that we might try them as we came to them. We soon found a cedar slab stuck up on which was written in charcoal:

"Fish Hear!"

The occupant of the first canoe which came along, not caring to make the experiment, and seeing his opportunity for a play upon words, added:

"*Do* Fish Hear?"

The next canoe, catching the joke, wrote:

"Do *not* Fish Hear?"

When the third canoe came up, the contents of the placard were read to the Indian, and his opinion asked. Looking round for signs of fish, he quietly exclaimed:

"Ugh! Fish *not* Hear!"

Although what was intended for a very different purpose had resulted in a novel discussion of a mooted question, it was decided that the very "bad spell" had reached a very wise conclusion.

For two weeks we were in daily telegraphic correspondence with Gen. ARTHUR, whose illness obliged him to return home after he had accompanied us as far as Bangor on our way hither. The character of his illness (which subsequently developed into a malignant carbuncle) rendered us uneasy, and our anxiety could only be appeased by these daily bulletins. A fatal termination of the malady was only avoided, under Providence, by careful home nursing and the best medical attendance, aided by a strong constitution and an indomitable will. The announcement of his hopeful convalescence was a pleasant piece of news, and when word came that he had "started for the Cascapedia," the Judge was eloquent in the expression of his gratitude and pleasure. But when one delightful Saturday morning he was seen in the distance snugly ensconced midships of his canoe, there was great joy in camp and preparations were made to give him a fitting welcome.

The Shedden pool, directly in front of the camp, had been left unfished for two days that he might enjoy it at its best. And it never "panned out" more richly than during the first afternoon he fished it. In five hours he landed four salmon, besides losing one through the stupidity of his gaffer, after a two hours' fight. They averaged twenty-seven pounds, the largest weighing thirty-pounds. With the capture of his first fish the last vestige of his illness left him. There is no medicine equal to the rise, strike and struggle of a thirty-pound salmon to bring back lost vigor to an appreciative convalescent.

The advent of the General among us was celebrated by the guides in the evening by a dance.

This was rendered possible, in due form, from the fact that one of the Indians was a violinist, and had his instrument with him. The lady of the neighboring farm-house kindly proffered her best room, and her three daughters were quite willing to join in the merry-making. It was a pleasant reunion, marked by all the decorum, with a thousand-fold the vivacity usually exhibited by the "first families" under like circumstances. The violinist was not a Paganini, but he kept perfect time with both elbow and heels. The Indians were very lively dancers, and the young ladies, by the ease and homely grace with which, in their tunic-like costumes, they followed the lead of their partners, gave evidence of long practice. If none of "the gentlemen" (as the guests were politely designated) "tripped the light, fantastic toe," it was from no discourtesy. The measured steps practiced in the *salons* of "society," compared with the hearty movements of these lusty dancers, would have been as monotonous as the dull thud of a muffled drum compared with the rattling thunder of a ponderous trip-hammer.

The dancing was interspersed with vocal music. Two of the young ladies sang, in duet, with exquisite taste and expression, that beautiful Scotch ballad, "I maun gang awa', lassie;" and the General, not to be outdone in courtesy, recited Burns' "Tam o' Shanter" and "Cotter's Saturday Night," in a most admirable manner, to the great delight of the venerable Scotch matron of the household and "ithers o' that ilk" who were present. The Judge also delighted every one by his good-humored rendering of that classically pathetic ballad, "Sam Jones, the fisherman," while DUN brought tears to the eyes of his susceptible audience by artistically chanting that profoundly plaintive ditty:

> "On Springfield mountains there did dwell,
> A comely youth I knew full well,"—

which "comely youth," it may be remembered, having been cruelly jilted, wandered off brokenhearted to die ignominiously from the bite of "a pesky sarpent."

In reportorial parlance, "nothing occurred to mar the festivities of the occasion," and all retired at an early hour the happier for having participated in the innocent hilarity of the evening.

CHAPTER XIX.

A SEARCH AFTER SOLITUDE.

How use doth breed a habit in a man!
The shadowy desert, unfrequented woods,
I better brook than flourishing peopled towns.
—[*Shakspeare.*

It may be laid down as a position which will seldom deceive, that when a man cannot bear his own company, there is something wrong.—[*Dr. Johnson.*

HAVING fished all the pools in the neighborhood of our main camp, I fancied that I could enjoy myself for a little while in a somewhat more primitive manner, alone, fishing some famous pools ten or twelve miles higher up the river. For, to tell the truth, our luxurious surroundings hardly comported with my early education in wood-craft, or with my ideas of the material elements which should enter into the camp-life of those who were even ostensibly "roughing it." Our commissary had assured us that it would be good for our general health to "live low on the river." But what a strange conception he had of low living! Delicious bacon, smoked ham, broiled salmon, fried trout, with occasional broiled spring chickens, tea and coffee, and oat-meal porridge with cream for breakfast! Canned ox-tail, chicken or turtle soup, with boiled salmon, roast or stewed lamb (fresh from a neighboring flock), plumb-pudding, with divers jellies, olives and pickles for dinner, and similar "rough" provender for our evening meal! Superadded to all this, tidy tents, with beds that wooed slumber like the music of the spheres, and thirty-pound salmon within casting distance, waiting to be "taken in out of the wet!" Can any of my old Adirondack companions wonder that I longed to exchange this sort of "rough" life for a day or two of fried pork and hard tack, a bark shanty and no conventionalities? And my Indian guide was quite as ready for the change as myself, in spite of the ten miles of hard pushing that was before him, and the assurance (which his past experience afforded him) that I would give him no rest during the expedition.

We left camp at eight o'clock, polled two miles and killed two salmon before half-past nine. It was an auspicious beginning, and the day closed with the capture of two more after we reached our destination, although six of the ten hours I was on the water were consumed in making the journey.

The "Upper Camp," as it is called, was not happily chosen It is pitched on a sandy promontory, closely enveloped on three sides by a dense jungle, from which a nervous sojourner might expect at any hour of the night a bear, wild-cat or moose to emerge. But it affords a perfect shelter from the winds, which often sweep down through the gorges of the mountains with fearful fury. It did so elsewhere on the river during my first night alone. At the main camp, the tornado was so severe that tents and shanties were in danger, and were only saved from demolition with the greatest difficulty; and it was as cold as it was tempestuous. But in my sheltered nook all was as quiet as if but a zephyr, instead of old Boreas, was dallying with the green leaves above me, and I sat in solitary state before my camp-fire in summer garments, while my friends ten miles off were pitying me for the discomforts I must be experiencing in my unsheltered cabin! So it is. Half the sympathy we expend upon others is wasted, either because the ills feared do not come to them, or because "the darkest cloud always has its silver lining."

These two days of isolation passed away very pleasantly. The weather was superb, the scenery magnificent and the sport all that I could desire. Only a single incident occurred worth special mention. In slowly drifting through an unpropitious looking pool, I made a cast or two at a venture, and unexpectedly hooked a fish of some twelve or fifteen pounds. As the canoe was moving when he rose, I struck him awkwardly, but he was fairly hooked. He showed his metal from the start. His first run nearly emptied my reel, and for half an hour he engaged in more curious pranks than any fish I had ever encountered. He literally "boxed the compass," and by his eccentric movements kept the canoe and myself in a perpetual whirl. I never had hold of a fish which seemed more determined to escape. The only possible way to prevent the line from running out was to follow him up, which we did, of course; but this required incessant "reeling in"—an exhausting piece of work, which becomes rather monotonous after a while. Tired and a little nervous, with the canoe and fish in constant motion, I was not prepared for the series of leaps which followed in such rapid succession as to be quite bewildering. One of these was of such unusual height that I was startled and neglected to lower my rod at the right moment. As a result he tore off! He had earned his liberty; and it seemed so impossible to master him that I scarcely regretted his escape.

I have, I believe, in a former chapter said something about the difficulty of acquiring the art necessary to save a leaping fish. There is seldom any danger in the ascent, because the line is then loosened and the expert angler instinctively recovers any slack that may result from this movement, so that by the time the fish is ready to descend, the line is taut; and unless this descent is followed by a simultaneous dropping of the tip of the rod, such a sudden strain on the line will ensue as to inevitably either break something or tear out the hook. The latter mishap was what befell me on this occasion. The hook had caught in some tender place in the mouth of the fish, strong enough to resist any ordinary strain but not strong enough to resist the pressure of a five or six feet plunge. No fish ever afterward leaped with my fly that my rod did not, in response, bow as promptly and as gracefully as the exigencies of the occasion required. No lesson is harder to learn, because nothing in all the angler's experience is so exciting as the spiteful leaps of a hooked salmon.

So, with the dashing rapids sparkling in the sun, with the balmy atmosphere redolent with the aroma of a thousand flowers, with the mountains casting their giant shadows upon the ever-changing landscape, with ten thousand birds warbling their grateful anthems, with no fretting cares or babbling intruders to jar upon the harmony of the scene, my ten-mile ride home was inexpressibly exhilarating. I can hope to experience no more ecstatic emotions until I stand upon the banks of that "pure river of water of life, clear as crystal," which sparkles in the sunlight of an eternal day.

While I had been thus reveling in solitude and enjoying myself to the "top of my bent," DUN and the Judge were rendered equally happy by the magnificent sport they had had in my absence. Each recounted his successes and mishaps before a rousing camp-fire, and the night was far advanced before the Judge wearied of describing, in his own inimitable way, the unpurchasable felicities available to a true angler on the banks of the "fair Cascapedia."

A day or two before my solitary ramble, an accident occurred on the river which might have resulted seriously, but which simply inconvenienced the gentlemen who were the unfortunate victims of it. I have before alluded to Mr. KINNEAR, of St. John, a veteran angler, and Capt. GRANT, of England, accomplished in all the mysteries of the art, who accompanied our party to the river, and who proceeded to the upper pools, thirty miles distant, to fish. They had with them most of their supplies for a fortnight, and their canoes were necessarily heavily laden. They had ascended several of the worst rapids in safety, and their Indian guides (two of whom had never before been on the river) had become less watchful than is essential to safety in these turbulent waters. The forward canoe, which was in charge of the two strangers, was being pushed up a very strong rapid, over one side of which a fallen tree projected. For a moment the canoe swerved from a direct course, was instantly driven backward with the speed of an arrow against this fallen tree, and went over like a flash, precipitating Mr. KINNEAR, his guides and all the luggage into the rushing waters. When Mr. K. came up (for at that particular spot the water is very deep) he found himself under the canoe, wedged in amongst the luggage; but he had the presence of mind to dive, and so extricated himself in time to prevent strangulation. It was a narrow escape, for which he was duly grateful. The occupants of the other canoes came to the rescue at the foot of the rapids where the water was not so deep, and succeeded in catching most of the luggage as it floated past. The canoe itself was badly broken, and it took two or three days to repair damages and to dry the saturated garments of the party. We had a visit from the captain, attired in Mr. KINNEAR's breeches; and as Mr. K. weighs two hundred and twenty, and Captain GRANT one hundred and fifty, the captain looked far less jaunty than when on parade with his crack regiment at home. But he enjoyed the mishap as an incident in his visit to the river.

Captain GRANT is a fine representative of the enthusiastic anglers of the old world. He has been a salmon fisher from his youth up, having taken his first lessons in Scottish waters so soon as he had acquired the muscle to make a cast. The passion had strengthened with his strength, and he had had the opportunity to gratify his tastes in all the most famous rivers in the four quarters of the globe. But in all his wanderings he found no waters so attractive as these. Whether in the East or West Indies — whether on the Tweed or Shannon — whether "at home" or in the jungles — his recollection of these salmon rivers was an ever-present and an ever-pleasant memory — the subject of his discourse by day and of his dreams in the night watches. And as proof of his enthusiasm he had twice crossed the Atlantic for no other purpose than to fish for salmon. The present season he took the steamer at Liverpool, landed at Farther Point, spent a month on the Restigouche and the Cascapedia, returned directly to Farther Point, and from thence home — only too happy to make a journey of six thousand miles to cast his fly in these magnificent salmon waters. Nor is his an isolated case. Many another of like tastes, and with a like appreciation of the kingly sport, every year make the same journey. All of these "simple wise men" may not be "princes in the king's household," but not one of them would assume the dignity of royalty itself if it involved the surrender of their prerogative at will to "go a-fishing."

CHAPTER XX.

A SHORT ESSAY ON FLY CASTING.

But, Johnnie, I maun, as ye'r frien', warn ye that it's no' the fly, nor the water, nor the rod, nor the win', nor the licht, can dae the job, wi'oot the watchfu' e'e and steady han', and a feeling for the business that's kin' o' born wi' a fisher, but hoo that comes aboot I dinna ken.—[*Donald Macleod, D. D.*

RDINARILY the waters of these salmon rivers are so transparent that in still pools long casts are indispensable to success. I make this qualification because great length of line is not so necessary in pools whose surface is broken by the current ripples, which serve the same purpose in a salmon pool that a sharp breeze does on trout waters—they blur the vision of the fish and render a more near approach feasible. But I never cast in either without parodying Napoleon's maxim: "Providence is on the side of the heaviest battalions:" success is on the side of the longest casts. I remember very well where I first learned this lesson. Many years ago, long before the North Woods became the fashionable resort of mere pleasure seekers, and while anglers still held the undisputed monopoly of their crystal waters, "Cole's Point," at the foot of Big Tupper, was one of my favorite resorts. Cast when I would, at early morning, at midday or in the gloaming, I was always sure of good sport. I would begin with a short cast, standing well back and dropping my fly at the very edge of the point around which the current, in those days, flowed with a graceful undulating motion over a cluster of bowlders where trout loved to congregate. For a few minutes I was kept busy, but the responses speedily ceased. By projecting my fly a few feet farther out, like results would follow; and so on until I had swept the entire length and breadth of the pool. Full half my take was from long casts. Why? Not because I had taken all the fish that were within easy reach when I began to cast, but because those I did not take, alarmed either by the shadow of my rod or the strugglings of the fish I hooked, slowly retreated, not really frightened, perhaps, but disturbed,—halting after a dart or two, to become themselves the victims of their ravenous appetite. If I had not followed them as they retired, I would not now have such pleasant recollections of "Cole's Point" as it was twenty years ago, before the dam at Setting Pole rapids had changed the whole surface of the Raquette waters below the Raquette falls.

As it is with trout so is it with salmon. When they are alarmed by the approach of your canoe, the glint of your paddle or the shadow of your rod, they do not rush from the pool, but they do what the leopard cannot do — they change their spots, retiring it may be fifty, eighty or a hundred feet from where your are anchored. If then you have the skill to reach them, you have a great advantage over those who have but half your skill. Hence my theory that success is always with the angler who makes the longest casts.

I once saw this very strikingly illustrated in a broad pool in which two friends were fishing at the same time. They were anchored on either side, and there was "ample space and verge enough" for both. But one could never get out more than sixty feet of line, while eighty or ninety feet was an easy cast for the other. With this exception, both were equally expert, equally enthusiastic and equally familiar with the habits and dainty tastes of their coveted prey. But the long cast scored two to his neighbor's one, because he had practically two-thirds of the pool. It is always thus, and hence every angler either for trout or salmon, should, if possible, acquire the art of giving his line a long sweep.

But some never acquire this art. Most novices start out with the idea that it simply requires the exercise of great muscular exertion to get out a long line. They lift their eight or ten ounce trout-rod as if they were lifting a sledge-hammer, and push it out with as much force as they would use to render the blow of a beetle effective. But no long cast was ever secured in that way. A quick but gentle movement, requiring scarcely more muscular exertion than the natural swing of the arm, is all that is necessary, taking care, however, that the line extends its full length backward before you force it to its forward movement. This is the simple single rule, by adhering to which, after reasonable practice, any one may make as long casts as are ever profitable. The same rule holds good in wielding the heavy double-handed salmon-rod, except that its greater weight requires greater exertion. But even here, length of line follows regularity of movement rather than muscular force, and yet without springy and well-balanced rods neither skill nor muscle will be of any avail. It is easier for me to cast eighty feet with one of my salmon-rods than fifty feet with another. In the one, every fibre, from tip to reel, seems instinct with life, while the other is as rigid and irresponsive as a hoop-pole. But, given a good rod and ordinarily skillful manipulation, no angler is excusable who cannot easily cast his trout-line sixty and his salmon-line ninety feet, where there are no obstructions within the radius of the cast.

No two anglers ever cast exactly alike. One gets out his eighty feet of line by a perfectly straight backward and forward movement of his rod. This is the most natural movement, the most simple, and generally the most effective. But in this movement, without a slight deviation from a straight line somewhere, there is always danger that your line or leader may, at some point in their journey, overlap. This danger is always imminent with a brisk breeze at your back. I do not, of course, invariably adhere to this movement,— never when the necessities of the case require a side cast; but where no material divergence from a straight line is necessary, I find it the most effective. Others give the rod its backward movement over the left shoulder and its forward movement over the right, or *vice versa*. This gives the line a graceful sweep which is not only artistic but avoids the danger of lapping. To make an equally long cast with this movement, however, requires greater skill than with the other; for, without the very nicest appreciation of time and distance, the curved sweep of the line will prevent it from acquiring the direct position indispensable to a perfect forward projection. But those who adopt this movement generally know what they are about. Indeed, the very best anglers of my acquaintance (notably Gen. Arthur) practice it altogether. Others invariably make the side or under cast, seldom lifting their rod above their shoulder. There are supposed advantages in such a movement, but I have never been able to discover them. One must have a large space of clear water to escape such entanglements with brush or tree-tops as no angler covets. Of course, there are times when this movement is necessary to enable one to reach desirable objective points, but it is not a movement to "tie to." Others still have no fixed mode of casting. It is their boast that they are equally expert in all. As a rule, however, you will find that in angling as in everything else, those who are "equally expert in all" rarely excel in any.

In casting, attitude may not be everything, but it is a great deal. And what a multitude of attitudes anglers assume! Some stand as erect as pillars, swaying neither to the right nor to the left, whatever reach of line they covet. Some sway to and fro, with every movement of their rod, like a tall pine in a tempest. Others throw themselves forward as if ambitious to follow their fly in person; while now and then one casts with an ease and grace of attitude and movement which would excite the envy and admiration of an athlete or sculptor. As I write, the recollection of one such comes back to me very pleasantly. He was an Adonis in form and *physique*, and his casting was the perfect "poetry of motion." Although like many of his contemporaries, his frosted locks and furrowed cheeks give token of advancing years, he still finds pleasure in the attractive pastime of angling. You have but to say to him, as Peter said to his disconsolate brethren, "I go a-fishing," to secure from him their response, "I go also."

But however one casts, it is impossible always to distinguish between the strike of a trout and that of a salmon; and as both are often found in the same pool, the angler is frequently annoyed by a call from the one when he is only eager to pay his respects to the other. The most experienced are often deceived, and they sometimes only discover their mistake after many minutes of exciting play. A four or five-pound trout (and trout of these weights are very common in these waters) can no more be hurried home than a twenty-pound salmon. The rod will only bear a certain pressure, and for a little while a five-pound trout reaches this point as unmistakably as the larger fish.

It was not until several days after it happened that Judge FULLERTON had the courage to relate an incident in his experience which goes to show how even a very wise man and a very expert angler may be deceived. He had been casting for some time without success, and was becoming impatient, when his fly was taken by a fish which ran off with his line as savagely as a forty-pound salmon would have done. The strike was magnificent, and the rush and resistance gave promise of a long fight. It was quite in vain that he tried to reel him in. The fish fought like a tiger, and not only compelled the Judge to frequently give him line, but rendered it necessary to follow him up to save the threatened tackling. So, through the pool he went on a run, then over the rapids with a rush, and down the swift water for half a mile, like a race-horse. His headlong movements were simply irresistible, and there was nothing for it but to follow his lead. So, the canoe and the fish dashed on together, the Judge in an ecstacy of delight with the magnificent play the gallant fellow was giving him. In the height of the battle, angler and gaffer pronounced him a twenty-pounder at least, and would have scorned to take off a single ounce from their estimate. And so the struggle continued for half an hour, hot and heavy, the Judge all aglow with perspiration and excitement, when the fish was brought to gaff, and came up *a five-pound trout instead of a twenty-pound salmon!* But "mum was the word!" and the gaffer was faithful to his promise. He gave no sign; and it was not until some others of us had related similar experiences that the Judge revealed this adventure with an imaginary twenty-pound salmon which turned out to be simply a five-pound trout.

CHAPTER XXI.

A FOREST PICTURE—AN UPSET IN "LAZY BOGAN."

There is, I think, a love of novelty in all anglers. We prefer to fish new waters when we can, and it is sometimes pleasanter to explore, even without success, than to take fish in familiar places. New and fine scenery is always worth finding.—[*W. C. Prime.*

HERE are a few pools on this river as on others, where an occasional salmon can be taken at any time from the first of June to the close of the season. Among these is the "Shedden pool," which is known as one of the very best between tide-water and the Forks. But after the middle of July, it is too near the sea to afford as rich returns as some others twenty or thirty miles farther up. It is salmon nature when started on their annual pilgrimage, to keep moving until they reach their maternal destination. On this river their chief spawning-places are from fifty to seventy miles from tide-water. But there are pools where they like to tarry on their journey; and we found none more generally thus honored than the pool referred to. Others might be "whipped" in vain, but this seldom failed to reward the patient angler, no matter when or how often it was visited. A monopoly of it for the season would afford any reasonable fisherman all the sport and pleasure he could desire, if he had no other object in visiting these waters than to fish. But they greatly mistake the temper and tastes of the true angler who assume that he is attracted to these quiet places simply to kill and to destroy. To have the opportunity to fish constitutes but one of the threads in the golden cord which draws him to the grand old forests in whose mountain streams trout and salmon "most do congregate." If he finds pleasure in the rise and strike and struggle of a mammoth fish, so also is he lifted up out of the rut of common-place emotions by his majestic surroundings — by the ever-shifting shadows on the mountain ; by the incessant music of the birds ; by the never-ending melody of the singing waters ; by the splash and foam and sparkle of the leaping cascade ; by the glinting sun-light upon ripple and rapid ; by the shadowy depths of the impenetrable forest ; by jagged rock and giant bowlder and dark pool and gliding river, and a thousand other "things of beauty" which remain upon the canvas of his memory long after the minor incidents of fish-taking are forgotten. No; it is not all of fishing to fish. That is but an incident in the angler's pleasant pastime. They have other and higher, if not more invigorating and exhilarating tastes to gratify. This beautiful picture of the poet is as often in their mind's eye as the rush and leap of the silver salmon:

> The trees are bursting into bud and bloom;
> The hills lie blue beneath a sapphire sky;
> The birds breathe music, and the flowers perfume;
> The pools lie placid as a maiden's eye.

I am sure that no one of our party would be content to visit any salmon river if they were restricted to such narrow limits as would afford them no variety in landscape, and no range for adventure. Quite as much pleasure is derived from experimenting in untried waters and in hunting up new bits of scenery, as in running up a great "score" to excite the admiration of partial friends or kindle the ire of envious rivals.

As the summer tourist often finds the most charming nooks by diverging from the beaten path, so does the angler often find the most attractive scenery by following up some half-hidden brook or rivulet which empties its crystal waters into the more majestic river which bears them to the sea. I had often fished the "Escumenack pool," which lies at the mouth of the river of that name, and had as often resolved to explore its hidden channel through the massive mountains amid which it has its source. So, one sunny afternoon my canoe was headed thitherward with as keen a relish for discovery as ever Columbus experienced while wearily waiting for royalty to launch him out upon unknown seas. And I had my reward in such a revelation of beauty as seldom comes to mortal vision. When we had pushed our way through some half mile of very swift water, we dropped into a natural basin of solid rock, whose picturesque surroundings constituted a fitting frame-work for the most charming and peaceful picture I ever saw. The water was from twenty to fifty feet deep, yet so transparent that the tiniest pebble was as clearly visible at the greatest depth as if held in the naked hand. What a pool for trout in their season! Now, however, not a fish revealed himself. I made a few casts, but without discovering any sign of life until my fly reached the rim of the basin, sixty feet distant, and then I only "flushed" a large trout, who refused my lure and moved off a few feet, as if disturbed by the unexpected apparition. But the water was so clear that I saw his every movement as he lay in seeming dread of what might befall him. In all my travels I never met with any water so perfectly transparent, or in which a minute object could be seen at so great a depth.

A few rods further brought us to the foot of the falls — a triplet of terraced cascades, combining as many points of beauty as Trenton, with more picturesque surroundings and as much to captivate the artist and excite the admiration of the appreciative lover of nature. They are seldom visited, even by anglers, because they are but little talked of. My Indian guide knew of them, but seemed to have no thought that any one would care to see them; and it was not until I announced my purpose to start out on a tour of observation that he informed me that I would find something that would reward me for my trouble. Hereafter, so long as I shall be permitted to fish in these waters, I will be sure to pay these falls a visit.

Similar bits of scenery are scattered all over this vast wilderness of forest, river and mountain. All the rivers have their sources hundreds of feet above the sea. The descent is not always made by a succession of rapids. At some points in most of them there are falls of no mean altitude, beyond which no salmon can ascend, and at the foot of which, in the season, they gather in fabulous numbers. There is such a gathering place on this river, seventy miles from the sea. We were within twenty miles of it, but such fearful stories were told us of the difficulty of making the ascent — of foaming rapids and jagged rocks, and probable shipwreck —

that we consoled ourselves with the reflection that it "wouldn't pay," the more particularly as our own knowledge of the river convinced us that the trip was only practicable during a higher stage of water than prevailed while we were in camp at the Forks. But I hope, before Providence shall shut me off from the Cascapedia, to behold the wonders which may be seen at this famous "summer resort" of the aristocracy of the sea.

In a recent letter I had occasion to mention a mishap which befell Mr. KINNEAR and Capt. GRANT. A similar incident occurred to Gen. ARTHUR soon after. He had been fishing "Lazy Bogan"— a famous pool in the vicinity of our camp — with indifferent success, when he deemed it advisable to change his base. To do so it was necessary to cross the stream at right angles with the current. Ordinarily this could have been done with safety, but unfortunately the General, with an eye to comfort, had placed a chair in his canoe, and in crossing, the frail craft careened under the pressure of the swift water, and this caused the chair to tilt and brought the General's two hundred pounds "avoir-du-pois" to such an angle as to cause the canoe to roll over "quicker than you could say Jack Robinson." The General, always submissive to constituted authority, promptly obeyed the law of gravitation, and was instantly submerged. But being a good swimmer, instead of ignominiously beating a retreat for the shore, he made for the canoe to prevent it, if possible, from passing down the rapids, to be there wrecked upon the rocks. But "Lo, the poor Indian," having either less courage or more discretion, made for *terra firma* with masterly "neatness and dispatch." And, as the sequel proved, it was well that he did, for as he was stoically watching the canoe and its submerged but self-possessed navigator, he saw the General's pocket-book gracefully floating down stream, and succeeded in clutching it. The fact that it was so light that it floated should be universally received as conclusive of its owner's official integrity. Indeed, but for this incidental evidence of his "honest poverty," it may be questioned whether he would have received the high honor of a unanimous vote on the question of his confirmation, for a second term, as Collector of the Port of New York. No other mischief resulted from this mishap than a thorough ducking, except that the General's watch stopped at the moment of the disaster, which was precisely eight minutes to seven, on one of the loveliest evenings of the year.

Something which might have been more serious occurred to myself while passing down one of the most impetuous rapids on the river. My Indian guide was in the bow of the canoe. He saw a dangerous rock ahead, and gave proper directions to the man in the stern, but his directions were misapprehended. The result was that while the one was trying to keep the canoe on the shore side of the rock, the other was doing his best to keep the rock on the shore side of the canoe. In this conflict of muscle the frail craft was rushing head-on to the rock at a speed of at least twenty miles an hour. The Indian saw the peril, and with a sweep of his paddle into which he seemingly put the strength of ten men, he succeeded in swinging the canoe inward, so that the bow just grazed the bowlder, while its bulging side came against it with a thud which, but for the elastic character of the birch bark of which it was constructed, would have smashed it into a thousand pieces. It was an anxious moment, for the water rushed downward amid a hundred other rocks with such force that only an expert swimmer could have got through in safety. The Indian was evidently in a white heat with rage, and so, from the fact that I never before heard him use an improper word, I hadn't the heart to chide him when he said: "Albert, don't you be damn fool any more!" And he wasn't. We shot through scores of rapids afterward (including the Indian Falls, the worst that I ever saw a canoe pass through and live) without a scratch. Nothing is more exciting, because nothing sane men ever attempt is more full of peril. If the king who offered a thousand pounds for a new sensation could have been induced to shoot one of these Cascapedia rapids, he would have had what he coveted.

CHAPTER XXII.

GOING UP THE RIVER — A THUNDER STORM — OUR CHAMPION MATCH-LIGHTER — EARLY MORNING FISHING.

Sir, you have angled me on with much pleasure to the Thatched House; and I now find your words true, that "good company makes the way short;" for, trust me, sir, I thought we had wanted three miles of this house, till you showed it to me. But now we are at it, we'll turn into it, and refresh ourselves with a cup of drink, and a little rest.—[*Sir Izaak Walton.*

IT was a beautiful summer morning when we broke camp at the "Shedden Pool" to visit The Forks, thirty miles distant. The change required the transportation of all our stores and camp equipage — ample lading for two baggage canoes, besides what could be carried in those occupied by the fishermen themselves. Our fleet of six boats "moved off in gallant style." Each canoe was propelled by two guides, and as they glided forward in "Indian file," to the steady music of their iron-tipped setting poles, the sight was quite inspiriting and picturesque. The ascent of the rapids was abundantly exciting, not only because great muscular exertion and skill were necessary on the part of the guides, but because it was often a matter of grave doubt whether the ascent could possibly be made. In the event of a failure, either from the force of the current or because of the divergence of the canoe from the proper line, nothing could prevent the frail craft from being hurled backward amid the huge bowlders which render the ascent or descent of the rapids always perilous. Accidents from either of these causes seldom happen; but there are occasional compulsory retreats and unpleasant upsets caused by the breakage or loss of setting poles or paddles at the most critical moment.

Upon one occasion my canoe had just surmounted a dangerous fall and was moving along in seeming security against the swift water a few rods above the crest of the rapids, when the setting poles of both my guides were caught in the clefts of the hidden rocks and snatched from their hands. The canoe was thus left to the mercy of the current. An upset seemed inevitable, and I instinctively began to disencumber myself for a cold bath. But in an instant both guides seized their paddles, and by almost superhuman exertions held their boat in proper line until it fell back upon the canoe in the rear, whose guides had caught up the floating setting poles and restored them to their owners. In the two minutes all this occupied there was concentrated as much excitement as one ordinarily experiences in a twelvemonth of quiet life. When, under the assurance of safety, the reaction came, I found myself as tremulous as if I had been wrestling with an athlete.

Our first ten miles were passed without any other adventure. But we were doomed to encounter one of those terrific thunder storms which are only met with in their grand and magnificent proportions in mountainous regions. It burst upon us with startling abruptness. The bright shining sun was suddenly obscured by heavy gray clouds, which came flying and rolling toward us as if propelled by a thousand tornadoes. These were followed by a troop of dense clouds black as night, from amid which there sounded out such peals of thunder as shook the huge mountains to their very foundations, and such incessant, sharp, quick lightning-flashes as "struck terror to the soul" of the most intrepid among us. The whole heavens were ablaze, and the almost midnight darkness which had thus unexpectedly fallen upon us was lit up as if by a limitless conflagration. And then were opened upon us the flood-gates of the skies, and we "took to the woods." The grouping of the drenched crowd as they sought shelter from the liquid avalanche was sufficiently ludicrous to excite boisterous merriment in spite of the bellowing thunder and the dazzling lightning, which rendered the roar and flash of ten thousand cannon the mere crackling of baby torpedoes. It was a grandly terrific spectacle, which amply compensated us for the delay and drenching which it brought to us.

We had hoped to make at least half our journey of thirty miles before night-fall. But the storm thwarted us, and the General cried "halt" when the twelve-mile land-mark was reached.

To those fond of it, camp-life, at its worst, has but few discomforts; but among these few none are more unpleasant than dripping leaves and saturated surroundings. After such a storm everything you touch is wet. The first thing coveted is, of course, a fire. But to find available material requires time and patient searching. And when found, where is the dry spot upon which to ignite a lucifer? In our party we had an expert to whom wind and weather had always hitherto presented no obstacle to the delicate manipulation required. Under the most adverse circumstances, it seemed only necessary for him to strike a well-defined attitude to secure the desired result. But upon this occasion the magic seat of his power had so gathered dampness that he scratched in vain, scratched he never so deftly; and when he found himself no longer "master of the situation," he was as indignant as was Balaam when his poor beast refused to do his bidding.

But the perplexities of fire-kindling in the woods after a rain storm, like other human ills, always have an ending. Very soon a glowing log-heap rendered our selected camping ground home-like and comfortable. The tents were pitched, the surroundings were speedily brought into ship-shape, a bountiful supper was prepared and eaten with a relish, the moon and the stars shone out resplendently, and after two or three hours of mingled sedate and merry conversation, stillness reigned supreme over the camp of a quartette of weary but happy anglers.

The morning after the tempest was all that heart could wish. The huge fire built in the centre of the camp had been kept in full blaze during the night, and dispersed every vestige of moisture within camp range long before any one not obliged to be moving cared to leave his comfortable couch. We had grown into the habit of taking things leisurely and were unwilling to break over a very pleasant custom simply because, by being tardy, we might fail to reach our destination before nightfall. I know that those who act upon the "early bird" theory may deem this confession derogatory to the character of zealous anglers. But I long ago abandoned the habit of fishing before breakfast, under the fallacious idea that neither trout nor salmon are ever so voracious as during the very early hours of the very early morning. A trout or salmon pool will yield just as handsome returns between the hours of eight and ten as between the hours of five and seven, if it remains undisturbed. A great many experts will probably dispute this statement; but if they will experiment as long and as faithfully as I have, they will agree with me, and by acting upon the discovery they will find themselves happier if not better men by contentedly enjoying their morning rest rather than encountering the raw morning air in their haste to secure the fish which would just as willingly and as surely come to them after breakfast.

In making the twenty odd miles which intervened between our extemporised camp and "The Forks," we encountered at least a dozen rapids which it seemed impossible that our canoemen could surmount. North Woods guides, with all their skill and intrepidity, would deem it absolutely necessary to "carry round" these formidable obstacles. And, with their boats, they would be obliged to do so. But these bark canoes seem just adapted to overcome these tumultuous waters. It is hard work, and requires a quick eye, a steady hand, a firm foot, and a wonderfully nice appreciation of the flow and force of the currents; but nothing seems so difficult as the exact balance they preserve during these great muscular exertions. They constantly change their setting poles from side to side and half face about with every change; but in doing so they preserve a perfect poise, not casting an ounce of improper weight upon either side while making these rapid changes. A novice, whatever props he might call to his aid, would find it impossible to maintain his equilibrium while passing either up or down these boiling cauldrons. But to lose his balance is the last thing to be apprehended from an expert canoeman. He has this art perfectly — acquired by long years of constant practice.

Indian Falls is by far the most threatening rapid on the river, and is the only one where anglers are expected to disembark in ascending. The canoes, however, are always polled up and it is very seldom that any accident happens. The descent is even more difficult, and prudent *voyageurs* take to *terra firma* rather than run the gauntlet of the numerous bowlders which dot the channel from summit to base. Only one of our party, however, had the good sense to "take to the woods" for half a mile rather than run the risk of a cold bath or something worse, by rushing down the fearfully turbulent waterway. It so happened that no harm befell his companions; but in making the detour he failed to share in the most exciting incident of the excursion. I have often passed the famous rapids of the St. Lawrence. That is an incident to be remembered and talked about for a life-time. But that passage is monotonous compared with shooting the rapids of Indian Falls in a bark canoe.

The river between the Falls and the Forks — nine miles — is comparatively still water, the current not averaging more than five or six miles an hour. The sail is delightful, and we enjoyed it to the full, reaching our destination just at nightfall. But it was midnight before any one was disposed to withdraw himself from the camp-fire, whose ruddy glow gave piquancy and breadth to the ceaseless flow of wit and wisdom which found ready utterance during these always pleasant evening hours on the banks of the "fair Cascapedia," the melody of whose singing waters never failed to quickly woo us to refreshing slumbers.

CHAPTER XXIII.

GRAND SPORT AT THE FORKS — LEAPING SALMON —
TORCH-LIGHT SURVEY OF THE POOLS.

And yf it fortune you to fmyt a gret fyfh with a fmall harnays thenne ye muft lede hym in the water and labour hym there tyll he be drounyd and overcome. Thenne take hym as well as ye can or maye, and euer be waar that ye holde not ouer the frengthe of your lyne, and as moche as ye may, lete hym not come out of your lyne's ende ftreyghte from you: but kepe hym euer vnder the rodde and euermore hold hym ftreyghte: foo that your lyne may be fufteyne, and beere his lepys and his plungys wyth the helpe of your cropp, and of your honde.—[*Treatyfe of Fyffhynge wyth an Angle*, 1496.

The clouds are silver in an azure sky;
  The hills lie basking in a sunny dream;
The lapping water coolly gurgles by
  Where lies the fallen trunk athwart the stream.

E first visited these upper waters of the Cascapedia last season. Our camp is fifty miles from the sea, and is "beautiful for situation." The spot chosen is a sort of peninsula, furnishing a fine view of the river and of the highest of the surrounding mountains. Our tents are pitched in the midst of a grove of young pines, whose shade is ample at all hours. The summer breeze has an unobstructed sweep from three directions, and nothing is lacking in tent or larder to render our temporary resting place an angler's elysium.

The early hours of our first day were full of forest music. An occasional bird whistled out his morning orisons. The murmur of the running water was pleasant to the ear, and the splash of the leaping salmon could be heard distinctly above the monotonous sough of the pines as they were waved to and fro by the balmy breath of the cloudless morning. What we knew of these pools rendered us impatient to test them, and much earlier than usual we were busy adjusting our rods and reels for the fray. To the curiosity which always accompanies the opportunity to cast in new waters was superadded the excitement caused by the salmon quadrille in full play within short pistol range of the camp. Every leap seemed a challenge, and gave promise of grander sport than we had yet experienced.

There was a good pool for each of us, and each proceeded in his own way to make the best use of his rare opportunity. The General had the first rise. All the signs indicated that he was fast to a fish of unusual weight. The initiatory rush and leap were prodigious, taking out nearly every foot of line and compelling a rapid forward movement of the canoe to prevent mischief. In a few moments the General was able to step out upon the pebbly beach, where he fancied he could the more successfully curb and capture his prey. For a while it looked as if he was about to demonstrate the soundness of his theory that a salmon fisher should always take to the beach where practicable, as soon as possible after he has hooked his fish. The tussle was severe and protracted. The fish was a stubborn brute, always doing just the very thing it was hoped he would not do — rushing and leaping and sulking in such eccentric and perverse ways as to keep his captor moving backward and forward like a wearied sentinel at his post. If the fish continued to thus turn upon his own tracks long enough, his capture, sooner or later, would be reasonably sure. But nothing is more uncertain than the movements of a hooked salmon, and those of us who had ceased fishing to witness the battle were not surprised when this lusty rascal made a dash down stream which soon brought the General to the end of his walk, and compelled him to take to his canoe to prevent the fish from making his escape; for you might as well try to hold a two-year old colt with a cotton thread as a rushing thirty-pound salmon by a direct pull on an exhausted line. It is for this reason that I always stick to my canoe during such a contest. You are better able to fol-

THE GENERAL FIGHTING A THIRTY-FOUR POUND FISH.

low where your fish leads. It would of course be different if wading were possible, but the water is generally too deep for that sort of fishing — altogether the most artistic and fascinating where practicable. As the General could not wade, he was forced to take to his canoe, which he did with great promptness and dexterity, but not an instant too soon. A delay of the twentieth part of a minute would have left him fishless and mortified. When thus again master of the situation, the contest was resumed by both parties with great vigor. No angler since the days of Nimrod ever played a fish more skillfully, or more fully enjoyed the exercise; but it was not until after a two hours' fight, extending over a distance of more than a mile, that he was brought to gaff. He weighed thirty-four pounds, and was the harbinger of many others like him captured in these pools during the period we remained at the Forks.

I repeated a hundred times during my first day here what the poet says of those athirst in mid-ocean: "Water, water every where, but not a drop to drink." The cause of this despairing cry on my part arose from the fact that while salmon were leaping all around me I could not, by any art or cunning at my command, lure one to my fly. At least twenty large fish were thus disporting themselves within easy cast, but no change of fly and no sleight in casting was of the least avail. They seemed impelled by mere exuberance of spirits. Sometimes I could see insects moving about in their neighborhood; but oftener nothing whatever appeared to justify or excuse their tantalizing friskiness. The novel spectacle, however, was entertaining, and was kept up for several hours without intermission. It is possible that some sort of fly would have lured them, but as nothing I had proved a success, I could only watch and wait. I tried to "jig" them — that is, to strike them with my hook while they were leaping, but I only succeeded in scratching the side of one of them as he was returning to his native element. This tantalizing sport continued so long that I had become weary of it, and I was ready to retire when one of the "gay gamboliers" took compassion upon me, and struck at my fly with such spirit as convinced me that I had some lively work before me. He was evidently quite as much surprised and startled as I was when he found himself under arrest. For when he first felt the sting of the hook he held himself as motionless as a log, as if cogitating upon the probable cause of the new sensation. But his cogitations were of short duration. Before I had time to up anchor and get properly braced for the encounter, he concluded to "go," which he did in the handsomest manner possible. He confined himself, however, to the pool, shooting back and forth with a rapidity and frequency which rendered it very difficult to keep a taut line upon him. I supposed, of course, that the disturbance would put a stop to the leaping which had been in progress through the entire morning. But it did nothing of the kind. While I was busy with my fish others were as busy jumping as before, and they continued to jump, often within a few feet of my canoe, during the whole of the protracted struggle. After a half hour's sulking, and a few vigorous attempts to break loose, he quietly succumbed. He was of medium weight — eighteen pounds — but he was only the forerunner of two others of more stately proportions that were brought to gaff before the going down of the sun.

The pool directly at the Forks — the intersection of the "salmon" and the "lake" branches of the river — should, from its position, be the very best between tide-water and the Falls. But it is not, probably because the pool itself changes with every spring freshet. Three of us had tried it faithfully in vain, and voted it barren, when DUN demonstrated his superior skill or luck by taking four fine fish from it after all the rest of us had utterly failed. It was neither the first nor the last time that his unwearied patience had its reward; and it was his patience quite as much as his skill which enabled him to generally lead all of us in the count. An essay on the advantages of this virtue, in every department of life, would be appropriate just here. But it would be a work of supererogation so far as my readers are concerned; for those who have followed me thus far through these rambling notes must possess the virtue in superabundance.

We had studied salmon pools in all their aspects, externally — their surroundings, their apparent depths, their currents, their counter-currents, their eddies and the particular spots within their circumference where salmon would be most likely to congregate. But we had never been able to peer down into their hidden depths to see the fish in their favorite haunts. To be sure, in passing up and down the river, now and then one would cross the vision like a silver ray. But, as a rule, they never came into view, even where we knew they lay in great numbers within easy cast. During the day they were hidden by the ripples caused by the currents and by the dark depths of the water, as securely as if they were "in the deep bosom of the ocean buried." There was but one mode by which we could obtain the view we coveted, to wit: by the use of the flambeaux, which the Indians use in their night-spearing forays, and by which, properly placed in the canoe, the water, to its lowest depths, becomes perfectly illuminated, and every object, to the tiniest pebble, is as clearly revealed as if it lay in the palm of your hand. But the use of the flambeaux is strictly prohibited by the laws of the realm. Aware of this, we took the precaution on coming in to secure a permit from the Warden to make a survey of the pools by torchlight, under pledge that we would destroy no fish during the process. As our object was simply to see the fish in their native element, and perhaps thereby learn something of their habits, we cheerfully gave the pledge and honestly intended to keep it.

The night chosen for this novel excursion was the last of our sojourn at the Forks. It was pitch-dark, and when our six canoes put out in Indian file, illuminated by a dozen flambeaux, the spectacle was exceedingly picturesque. The dense forest loomed up grandly in its impenetrable vastness. The surface of the river seemed a bed of molten silver, and the Indians, as they stood up with setting pole or paddle, looked weird and ghost-like. Starting from the upper pool, we floated down more than a mile, salmon at every step showing themselves, shooting hither and thither, aroused from their repose by the unusual spectacle. Scores of fish were seen in pools where we had cast in vain; and even in shallow, swift water, where we never thought of casting, they appeared in large numbers. So long, however, as we continued to float with the current, the view was unsatisfactory, except in revealing an abundance of fish. We could get no quiet look at them; they appeared and disappeared like a flash. We, however, had as favorable an opportunity as we could desire when we passed into the still water of "Lazy Bogan"— a bayou at the head of the very best pool on the river. This bayou is full of deep holes, with clear sandy bottom. Each of these still pools was filled with salmon, and as we held our boat above them, we could see them perfectly, gracefully moving about and with such deliberation as to afford us just the view we desired. We saw in this still water, where they are not supposed to ordinarily resort, at least fifty, of all sizes, ranging from ten to forty or fifty pounds. It was a sight worth a journey hither, and it will never be forgotten.

I said we gave our pledge that no fish should be killed during our survey. In starting out we peremptorily enjoined our guides not to strike at the fish, under penalty of our gravest displeasure; and they promised. But they did not keep their promise. The moment the schools of fish appeared they became wild with excitement, and, in spite of our constant reminders, they would strike out with gaff and pike-pole in a perfect frenzy of delight. They kept up a constant shout of "There they go!" "Salmon!" "See there!" "Look! Look!" accompanying every cry with a thrust of their pike-pole or paddle, as if they were the spears with which, before the laws interposed, they were wont to fill their canoes during their night forays. Fortunately, only two fish were hit — one with a pike-pole, thrown out as a spear, and another scooped up with a gaff while boat and fish were both in rapid motion. This latter achievement was hailed with shouts of delight by all the Indians, and Jack, by whom the extraordinary feat was performed, held the struggling fish high above his head, while thus impaled, exclaiming as he did so: "Ah! ha! what you say now? who the best gaffer, eh? what Indian can beat that, eh?" No champion of the ring ever manifested greater delight when awarded the belt than did Jack when he gaffed this salmon on the wing. We were mortified and angered, of course, that our peremptory orders had been, in these two cases, disobeyed; but we could not but admire Jack's skill, and enjoy the exhibition of Indian character which found expression during this exciting and never-to-be-forgotten flambeaux visit to the salmon pools of the Cascapedia.

It is only proper to say that we reported this illegitimate killing of two salmon to the Warden on our return, explaining the circumstances and expressing our mortification and regret. We proffered every reparation in our power, in the way of humble apology or pecuniary penalty, but we had not the heart to name the real delinquents; for we could not but believe that they were so beside themselves with excitement that they could not have been restrained by any authority. The Warden, of course, admonished us, as was his duty, but kindly consented to overlook the delinquency in view of the frankness of our confession and the circumstances under which the delinquency occurred.

CHAPTER XXIV.

A BEAR CHASE — A GOLD HUNTER — TACKLING FOR SALMON FISHING.

I had a glimpse of him, but he shot by me
Like a young hound upon a burning scent.
— [*Dryden.*

Know'st thou not any whom corrupting gold
Would tempt into a close exploit of death?
— [*Shakspeare.*

DEER were at one time very abundant in this region, but merciless hunting at all seasons has either extinguished or driven them to other feeding-grounds less accessible to their inhuman enemies. It is, however, the Bears' paradise. They seem to have a *penchant* for the sheepfolds lying on forest borders. Every farmer considers a bear-trap as necessary as a plow, and captures are frequent.

Our first camp was in the neighborhood of several farms where bruin had marauded successfully. DUN, being the most ambitious hunter in the party, was in constant expectation of an opportunity to prove himself as skillful with the rifle as with the rod. In the pursuit of minor game he had found "a foeman worthy of his steel" in Judge FULLERTON, whose eye is as keen as his wit, and who bags his game as expertly as he extracts truth from a reluctant witness. The two were well matched. Some of their contests for the championship "astonished the natives," and would have secured them backers for the proposed international "shoot" at the Centennial. Both of them had "slain their thousands" of every living thing, from chipmunk to deer, but neither had ever fleshed his maiden bullet in a bear. Both hoped and waited; but DUN had the advantage in that he was the owner of the only rifle in camp, and made it his constant companion.

He had begun to despair of a chance to bring a bruin to book, when, while quietly enjoying his after-dinner pipe, a tiny dug-out was seen gliding rapidly across the river from the farm-house directly opposite, its occupant shouting lustily, "A bear! a bear!" This was the signal DUN long had waited for, but feared he'd die without the sound. The effect upon him, as upon all of us, was electrical. In an instant he was in the dug-out, accompanied by myself as his henchman.

The moment we struck the shore our excited guide led off on the trail with a speed which would have been creditable in a retreat, but which was bad generalship in an advance upon such an enemy. The foolish fellow did not seem to understand that his followers had neither his wind nor his muscle, and that, without a little practice, it was quite impossible to ascend a precipitous mountain-side at a two-forty pace, even though a bear's scalp might be the prize awaiting us at the end of the race. We had run four or five hundred yards at our best speed, when our guide, far in advance of us, yelled out, "Here he is! here he is!" in such thunder-tones as would have "struck terror to the souls" of a thousand bears, had they been in the neighborhood. The cry, however, was inspiriting. Although DUN was already "blowed," the heralded proximity of the enemy gave him new life, and he scrambled forward, rifle in hand, with an energy which lifted him in my estimation to the dignity of an exhaustless wind instrument. For myself, I could only lie down and pant. On sped DUN, however, like an Indian runner, determined to have that bear's hide or die for it. But luck was against him. As the guide yelled out, "There he goes!" I saw the beast rise the brow of the hill and scamper out of sight, unscathed. But my discomfitted friend had had "a good drive out of him," and but for the stupidity of the excited bumpkin, he could have achieved his life's ambition. It only required a cautious approach; for at the first alarm, the bear was quietly feeding upon the carcass of a sheep, and would have continued his repast until gorged, had he not been disturbed.

Moose are still numerous, but at this season are generally far back in the mountains. An occasional straggler, however, finds his way into the valleys. Their tracks are seen everywhere along the river, but it was our fortune (last year) to see but one in motion. He was fording the river two or three hundred yards below our camp at the Forks, and but for the tumult made by our excited Indian guides, he could have been bagged. As it was, he escaped, a rifle ball following him at random as he passed into the woods. He was about the size, color and shape of a Jersey cow.

Moose, like deer, have been hunted unmercifully, and are by no means as plentiful as they were twenty years ago, when it was an easy matter to kill a dozen in a week within ten miles of our present encampment. Their threatened extermination induced the enactment of very stringent laws for their protection; and as such laws are more respected here than by the "free and independent electors" on our own borders, within a few years moose, like salmon, will be as plenty as in their palmiest days.

Of small game, duck are most abundant. In

passing up and down the river, you intercept broods at every turn. The cunning shown by the mother bird in its efforts to divert attention from her young is an interesting study. The maternal instinct is quite as strongly illustrated in them as in any other game-bird known to the sportsman.

The monotony of our camp was one day broken by a visit from a gold seeker, who had faith in an Indian tradition of "a mountain of gold" near the head-waters of this river. The story goes that some fifty years back an old Indian came into the settlement with several heavy lumps of the precious metal which he exhibited to a trader as specimens of an inexhaustible supply of "the same sort," available to any one who would take the trouble to dig for it. The trader pronounced the specimens worthless, but succeeded in getting possession of them nevertheless. In his cupidity, however, he refused to return the Indian an equivalent for his prize; and, in revenge, the red man refused to reveal the locality of the placer, and as he died one day, the secret died with him. It was said, however, that when beside himself with the "fire-water" of the white man, he so far indicated the neighborhood of the hidden treasure as to induce, twenty-five years ago, a company of credulous white men to search for it. Our present visitor, then quite young, was one of the party. They discovered signs of gold, they thought, and glittering particles that looked like gold, but they had only "their labor for their pains." Since then this young man had been in California and had acquired an experience which he believed would render his present search a success. He had chemicals with him to test the "golden sands" of this new El Dorado, and he pushed on, full of high expectations. But, alas! for the mutability of all human hopes, he returned in six days a disappointed man. He succeeded, he said, in getting within five miles of the golden mountain, but his *high-heeled boots* behaved so badly that he could not prosecute his search! The Indians who accompanied him said he became frightened. But, however that may be, he certainly failed, and had his journey from the far West to the head-waters of the Cascapedia for nothing. He returned, like many another gold-seeker, the victim of misplaced confidence. There are those who still have faith in this old tradition, and the search will be kept up so long as unreasoning credulity remains to vex the race.

Before "reeling up" these disjointed and wearisome notes, as I shall do very soon, it may not be deemed out of place to proffer just a word of counsel to those who may, at some not distant day in the golden future, have the happiness to "go-a-fishing," if not in the Cascapedia, in some other of the multitude of rivers where salmon gather.

Happy beyond his fellows is the angler who has the skill to "fix up" his own tackling, to tie his own flies, to properly adjust his own reels, to make up his own leaders, and to do whatever else is necessary to be done to render him superior to calamity and independent of all ordinary mishaps. It took me many years to acquire this skill and more years to command the leisure to render it available. But even now, I am often obliged to call in the aid of experts to do for me what (if I could) I would find great pleasure in doing for myself. The finest salmon-flies I ever saw were made by our recent townsman, DEAN SAGE — an expert in all the intricacies of the art, and the possessor of all the high qualities and gentle virtues of the noble guild of anglers. Judge FULLERTON, of our party, also possesses this desirable gift of deftness in large measure. If he had turned his attention to mechanics instead of the law, he would have become quite as eminent as an artisan as he now is in the profession he adorns.

My experience of last year, or rather the experience of others — for I was unusually exempt from accidents — taught me that it is never safe, where the fish sometimes reach the weight of forty pounds, to rely upon a single rod, line or reel, however excellent. They should always be held in duplicate. One is apt to be over-timid who has nothing to fall back upon in case of breakage; and nothing is more fatal to success and nothing more unpleasant than the constant fear that an extra pressure may snap things and exhaust one's resources. The best of tackling and plenty of it is the only safe rule. If, as in my case, no breakage happens, you will still have the satisfaction of knowing that you are prepared for the worst. My rod and line of last year served me through this, although my three hours and twenty minutes fight with my last fish caused such a perceptible weakening of one joint of my rod as to indicate that a few more such struggles would cause a rupture. I would sincerely regret such a calamity, for, by the verdict of every expert who has handled it, as well as by the verdict of my own experience, a better salmon-rod, in strength and elasticity, never responded to the cast of an angler. And yet it is one of the plain sort, of medium cost and beauty, like some fast steppers you occasionally meet with, "nothing to look at but great to go." It springs, with mathematical exactness, from tip to butt, and only requires the gentlest effort to launch out a sufficient cast to cover any pool of ordinary circumference. Two of our party had superfine split bamboos, upon whose construction as much skill had been displayed as money could command; but they both discarded them, after faithful and fatal trial, for rods the counterpart of my own, with the most satisfactory results. And yet there are those who prefer the bamboo; and some of the best anglers of my acquaintance use no other. But all bamboo rods are not alike any more than all rods of solid woods. The handsomest rod I ever owned, of foreign make at that, and which was pronounced by all who ever examined it to be as good in quality as in looks, proved to be worthless. After using my favorite rod, it was like casting with a hoop-pole, and has taught me, what all men are taught sooner or later, never to trust to appearances, either in fishing-rods or men.

CHAPTER XXV.

DOWN THE RIVER — RUNNING THE RAPIDS — A WORD OF WARNING — HOMEWARD BOUND.

And now, scholar, with the help of this fine morning and your patient attention, I have said all that my present memory will afford me. * * But I shall long for the month of May; for then I hope again to enjoy your beloved company at the appointed time and place. And now I wish for some somniferous potion that might force me to sleep away the intermitted time, which will pass away with me as tediously as it does with men in sorrow; nevertheless I will make it as short as I can with my hopes and wishes. * * These thoughts have been told you that you may also join in thankfulness to the Giver of every good and perfect gift, for our happiness. * * So, scholar, I will stop here.—[*Sir Izaak Walton.*

OUR week's sojourn at the Forks passed away "like a tale that is told;" but its memory, like "a thing of beauty," will remain to us "a joy forever." It was an uninterrupted carnival of pleasure. If all nature had combined to minister to our happiness, we could not have been made more supremely content; and in a spirit scarcely less devout than that which moved the Psalmist, we often exclaimed, "Our cup runneth over;"

"surely mercy and peace hath followed us all the days of our" sojourn in these quiet places.

The morning after our torch-light review of the salmon pools was cloudless and serene. The grand old forest seemed the temple of silence. The air was full of the sweet odors of pine and wild-flowers, and the early morning light came down through the dense foliage like a divine benediction. The pleasant murmur of the running waters, blending with the plaintive chirp and whistle of the wood-bird, went down into the heart like the still small voice of the Spirit, awakening tender emotions of gratitude and thanksgiving. To the devout mind, these vast forest-temples are the best types of that other temple "not made with hands, eternal in the heavens," whose ineffable glories are yet to break upon the enraptured vision of the redeemed.

The sun was just scattering his golden dust upon the green foliage which gives beauty to the rugged summit of "Big Berry Mountain," when the General issued his order to embark. It was hard to say "good-by" to a place where we had enjoyed so many days of superb angling and so many evenings of joyous camp-life. But the tenth of August — the end of our permit, and practically, of the fishing season — had arrived and we must needs go home. So, with a sigh and a farewell to this place of pleasant memories, with a salute from our only rifle and a cheer from all of us, we swept out into the swift current, and were "homeward bound."

What a contrast to our tedious ascent was this seaward journey! Our light canoes glided through the water like birds in the air. Although there are many "stretches" unbroken by rapids, there is no point on the river, from its source to tidewater, where the current does not move quite four miles an hour. The first nine miles were mostly of this quiet character, and it is impossible to conceive of anything more delightfully exhilarating than the movement through such waters on such a morning as that in which we made the journey. It was the very poetry of motion. The sun was without a cloud; the air was just of the temperature one would like to bask in forever; the foliage still sparkled with the dew of the morning; the mountains were aglow with sunlight, while midway of their summits the early mists hung in great silvery masses, forming pictures which dwarfed the grandest handiwork of man, and awed us with their vastness, their grandeur and their indescribable beauty. Every bend of the river revealed some new landscape to admire, while the chirp and whistle and song of ten thousand wood-birds found responsive melody in our own glad hearts. It was no surprise to me that my companions gave occasional expression, in shout and song, to their ecstatic emotions; and if I responded in kind, it was simply because it was quite impossible to refrain from giving some audible token of my entire sympathy with them. It is not often one reaches such a condition of mind and body as to find himself in perfect accord with the poet:

> One sip of this
> Will bathe the drooping spirits in delight
> Beyond the bliss of dreams.

Such moments, however, occasionally come to every one of us, but never more impressively than when surrounded by the sublime and beautiful in nature; when enveloped in an atmosphere charged with the very elements of perpetual youth, serene and balmy as the breath of God. Where more than in the solitudes of the forests are these emotions likely to come to the spirit of the thoughtful and devout? The Psalmist had a glimpse of what was attainable amid such surroundings, when he exclaimed:

> "Oh, that I had wings like a dove! for then would I fly away, and be at rest.
> "Lo! then would I wander far off, and *remain in the wilderness.*"

In six hours we compassed the distance which required two days of hard work to accomplish when moving against the current. The flight down the numerous rapids was intensely exciting. It requires a quick eye and a steady hand to run the *chute* in safety. But accidents are rare. The Indian guides, who were born on the river, are as familiar with every hidden bowlder and every dangerous eddy as the denizen of the city is with the pathway to his place of business, and they take their canoes safely through channels where, if directed by the uninitiated, they would be inevitably dashed into fragments. As a rule, it is perfectly safe to go where an Indian is willing to take you. He has just that sort of discreet courage which leads him to keep as far from danger as possible; and he will never take his canoe into waters he is not quite sure he can safely navigate. I only once insisted that my guide should go through a channel which he pronounced unsafe. He obeyed orders under protest, wondering at my foolhardiness and temerity. The result of the experiment may have given him a favorable opinion of my courage, but I am sure it depreciated his previous estimate of my good sense. The sensation was somewhat thrilling as we dashed through the boiling cauldron, but it was purchased at the expense of saturated garments and a half-filled canoe. But for the almost superhuman efforts of the faithful fellow we would have been inevitably swamped, if not badly bruised and battered by the jagged rocks which everywhere show themselves in the midst of these impetuous rapids. I never again asked my Indian to take me where he didn't wish to go himself.

After a short stop at our first camp, the capture of a few more salmon in Shedden pool, and the proper packing of our camp equipage to be in readiness for our hoped-for visit next June, we "reeled up" and were off. We had had a month of rest and enjoyment such as can only be attained in the solitudes of the forest and on a river famous for the magnificence of its scenery and the size, vigor and kingly character of its fish.

And just here, in closing up these rambling sketches, it may be proper to remind some of my readers of the old adage that "what is one man's meat is another man's poison." It is not conclusive that because angling, with its pleasant concomitants, affords the highest pleasure to the few, that it would be found equally attractive to the many. It may not be true to the extent assumed by good old Sir Izaak, that to become an expert angler or a true poet, one "must be born so." But it is true that peculiar tastes are necessary to the full enjoyment of any special pastime. The man who is only happy in a crowd, would soon become tired of the stillness and solitude of the forest. He who finds his chief pleasure amid the luxuries and ornamentations of artificial life, would speedily weary of the cloud-capped mountain, the shadow of the woods, the melody of the singing waters, the cheery *abandon* of camp-life, the informal and unostentatious courtesy and pleasant conversation of the "simple wise men" who find delectation in these quiet places. Every angler has melancholy memories of this fact — the recollection of many spoiled vacations by reason of the uncongenial companionship of "dear friends" who had mistakenly fancied that what gave pleasure to others could not fail to contribute to their own happiness. But on trial, instead of pleasure they found only *ennui;* and by their evident discomfort they rendered every one about them as miserable as they were themselves. And this, not because they were not *au fait* in all the courtesies and proprieties of social life, nor yet because they were indifferent to the happiness of others, but simply because their tastes were not in harmony with their surroundings, and so were disappointed in the realization of their high anticipations.

I would, therefore, recommend no one to seek pleasure from a protracted sojourn in the woods, either with rod or rifle, until he tests his tastes by brief excursions. If he so enjoys a few days "under canvas" that he longs for a repetition of the pleasure, he may reasonably hope that a month on a salmon river would not be tedious. But, as you regard your own comfort and the comfort of others, do not assume that, because your friend finds his highest pleasure in the practice of the gentle art, you also must needs be happy in its pursuit.

To give variety to our trip we took carriages from New Richmond for a thirty-mile ride along the borders of the Bay of Chaleur; and we enjoyed it greatly. Almost the whole distance is a continuous village, and nearly all the houses are the abodes of men who make a precarious living by catching and curing codfish for the markets of the world. For more than a hundred and fifty years this has been the chief occupation of all the residents of this coast. The result is extreme poverty and — contentment. The men of to-day live and labor as their fathers had done through many generations. This, however, can be said for them — they are the most polite people on the continent. Meet whom you would, man or boy, on foot or borne along in his rickety cart or jaunty calash, no matter, you were sure of a graceful greeting. During our ride of thirty miles, in no single instance was this act of courtesy forgotten. It was a custom I had met nowhere else in all my wanderings.

Taking the steamboat at Paspebiac, we had a

pleasant two days' sail through the Gulf of St. Lawrence to Quebec, thence by rail to Montreal and home — grateful for what we had enjoyed, and hopeful of the return of another season when we shall again be able to "go a-fishing."

Trout Fishing in the Adirondacks.

CHAPTER XXVI.

VISIT TO THE ADIRONDACKS IN 1873 — WHEN TO FISH — A STATE PARK — FOREST MEDICINE.

Angling is somewhat like poetry: men are to be born so—I mean with inclinations to it, though both may be heightened by discourse and practice. But he that hopes to be a good angler must not only bring an inquiring, searching, observing wit, but he must bring a large measure of hope and patience, and a love and propensity to the art itself. But having once got and practiced it, then doubt not but that angling will be so pleasant that it will prove to be, like virtue, a reward to itself.—[*Sir Izaak Walton.*

I HAVE discovered that many beside experts take pleasure in reading whatever is said in praise of angling. They have the good taste to appreciate a healthful amusement which they have not the leisure to enjoy. I made this discovery many years ago, when I began a series of letters from "The Woods," which I kept up without intermission until that summer of disasters when McClellan led so many of our brave boys to defeat and death. It seemed like mockery to draw pleasant pictures or speak of personal enjoyments when the whole nation was in tears, when ten thousand Rachels were weeping for their children, and when the shadow of death hung like a pall over the whole land. So, from that time to this I have made no record of these delightful excursions. Although I have been thus silent for so many years, with the exception of a single summer (of sad memory), I have been permitted to enjoy my month's sport, always awaiting its coming with longing, and always entering upon it with new zest and ever-growing pleasure.

It was weary waiting this year for "the time of the singing of birds" to come. The spring was more backward than for twenty years. The snow lingered in the woods until far on in May, and it was not until the middle of the month that experienced anglers deemed it worth while to wet their lines in any of the waters of the Adirondacks. For be it known to all novices in the art, and to all who hope to become used to the ways of trout, and experts in their capture, that the best sport only comes after the snow-water has disappeared and the streams have acquired their natural clearness and placidity. High water is not desirable, even for spring fishing; but it is not fatal to success. One has only to know the ground he traverses, and the best points at different seasons, to gather success even with full banks; but a flood is not to be coveted. The best results are attainable in the spring when the water is falling, and in the summer when it is rising. I have fished in vain in August through a whole day, at the outlets of favorite streams, where, after a rain, I have taken trout in great numbers. A sharp summer shower, by raising the brooks, brings down the feed from the upper waters, and the trout, who know when it rains as well as the angler, concentrate to gather the harvest sent to them. He is fortunate who is at hand to avail himself of such occasions.

In all this region the ice usually disappears from the lakes between the middle and close of April, and I have sometimes started out on the first of May to begin my spring's fishing. But this year it was the 9th of May before the ice succumbed, and the 15th found the snow still intact on the shaded hill-sides and through all the valleys. It was tedious waiting; but there is an end to all things, even to a tardy spring and the chilling relics of a long winter.

As soon as the ice leaves, you may hope for success in trolling. Lake-trout are a gamey fish, and their capture affords exciting sport to those who like it; but it has always seemed to me monotonous and unartistic. Given a proper length of line, weight of sinker, strength of rod, and an intelligent guide, an expert seems to have no advantage over a novice, except in the single act of landing the fish after he strikes. Unlike fly-fishing, it affords no muscular exercise, no constantly recurring excitement, no skillful casting, no delicate manipulation, and none of the thrill which follows the rise and rush of the fish for the lure which rests upon the surface of the water. And yet it is a pleasant pastime, healthful and invigorating, affording ample opportunity for reading and meditation, and bringing before the eye ever-changing views of the grand old mountains and forest-clad valleys which constitute the attractiveness and beauty of all this region. When the "grasshopper shall become a burden," when "those that look out of the windows shall be darkened," when "the keepers of the house shall tremble," when my "right hand shall forget its cunning," and when I shall no longer be able to wade the mountain stream or cast a fly, if Providence shall thus gently lead me homeward, I shall doubtless find delight in this less robust and less exhilarating amusement. But, meanwhile, I shall leave the troll to those whose waning vigor, neglected education, immature tastes or blissful ignorance render them content with this primary branch of the angler's art.

The "signs" which mark the advent of the "good time" longed for through seven months of weary winter and tardy spring — the budding of flowers and the blossoming of fruit-trees — having come, with a single companion, and with an elastic buoyancy not at all in keeping with the traditional rheumatic propriety of time-wrinkles and silvered locks, we moved off, on the 23d of May, for that Eden of Anglers, where nature unadorned excels in picturesqueness and grandeur, as well as in vastness and magnificence, all the noted parks and preserves which have acquired their attractiveness and beauty through the genius, taste and affluence of man. And I trust that this vast forest may never be less a forest than it is to-day. The movement recently initiated to declare it and hold it in perpetuity as a state park, marks the wisdom of those who made the suggestion, is in harmony with the spirit of the age, and, a century hence, if now inaugurated, will be recognized as the highest proof of the wisdom, sagacity and foresight of the statesmen of our time. And this not simply because it would thus remain forever a resort for the sportsman and invalid, but because it would remain forever, as it is to-day, the abundant feeder of several of our navigable rivers, and the best guarantee, as science assures us, of that equable temperature and uniform rain-fall which are so essential to the material prosperity of the State. The arguments in favor of the proposition are irresistible to all but those who contemn the logic of science and " take no thought" for the generations to come, who will follow us with their blessings or their maledictions according as what we project or accomplish is petty and injurious or grand and beneficent.

Many wonder that veteran anglers so often enter this vast solitude alone, or with but one or two companions. The answer is easy. It is impossible for men of radically dissimilar tastes in minor matters to always enjoy each others' companionship in the compulsory intimacy of camp-life. The slightest exhibition of uneasiness, discontent or impatience is sufficient to cast a shadow upon the whole camp, and excite perpetual apprehension lest the programme of the day shall run counter to the wishes of some of "the crowd." One who goes into the woods to find a respite from the rasping collisions of business or professional life, does not like to encounter disharmonies in the very solitude where he had thought to find repose. It would not be difficult to pick up a score of good fellows, enthusiastic anglers and excellent companions; but it would be difficult to find half that number who would be always in harmony on the minor points of camp-life. There are some who desire to be always moving and others who are satisfied wherever the surroundings are pleasant and fishing tolerable — who are content with the poorest "luck," and who find their highest enjoyment in killing trout in the most improbable places.

It was not until the 25th of May that the budding flowers and fruit-tree blossoms gave token that the time had come when one might hope for success in angling in these prolific waters. It was a pleasant day, clear and sunny, just such a day as one likes to have when starting out upon a journey, whether of business or of pleasure. A brief run to Whitehall, and a quiet night-ride through Lake Champlain brought us to Plattsburg, the gate-way to the wilderness.

The road from thence to the Saranac lake, twenty miles by rail and thirty-five by wagon over a fair road, opens up a constant succession of grand mountain views, making the ride one of the most agreeable and picturesque to be found within the compass of the State.

Martin's hostelry, which has been quadrupled in dimensions since I first visited it fifteen years ago, is located at the foot of the lower Saranac, and is one of the two or three really excellent resting-places in the wilderness. My only present objection to it is that it too much resembles, in its service and appointments, the "first-class" hotels of our more fashionable watering-places. But so we go. No sooner do we find a pleasant place where we can literally "take mine ease in mine inn," and walk about, if one so pleases, in slippers and shirtsleeves, than presto, silk trails, patent-leather boots and kid gloves drive us elsewhere to find simple comfort, unincumbered by stately formalities and white cravats. But Martin deserves the prosperity he is enjoying; and he knows so well "how it is himself," that he always reserves "space and verge enough" in his ample mansion to permit the unostentatious and quietly disposed angler to enjoy himself in his own way without disturbing the less simple-minded guests who come hither to breathe the pure mountain air and renew their youth.

Notwithstanding the nonsense Murray and others have written about the beneficent influence of a trip through the Adirondacks upon the health of hopeless invalids, the real invalids — those who require home-like repose as well as change of air — have generally too much good sense to believe that an exhausting journey, exposed to all sorts of weather and to inconveniences and hardships unbearable without very considerable vitality, can, by possibility, be beneficial. To be sure, the year succeeding the publication of Murray's book, not a few, standing on the very brink of the grave, were deluded into the hope that, if they could but manage to drag themselves or to be dragged from the Saranacs to the Fulton range, they would, by some undefinable process, experience the miracle of a resurrection. But after a few had suffered miserably and others had died in the effort, the delusion vanished, and now the very sick wisely conclude that while the pure atmosphere of this region is of real service, it has no such miraculous power as has been attributed to it. They find that to be benefited by it they must seek the comfort and repose of a well appointed dwelling rather than the discomforts and inconveniences of camp-life, and that where there is serious illness, "there is no place like home." In the initiative of disease, when the system is enervated by overwork of muscle or brain, it will derive lasting benefit from a summer's sojourn here. But it would be far better if those thus suffering should make this pilgrimage before, rather than after, their malady becomes chronic.

I had never before been so late in my spring trip to the woods. But I knew too much of the habits and haunts of the trout to waste my time by calling upon them before their house was in order or before they were in the humor to give us a cordial reception. On reaching Martin's, I found a score of disappointed fishermen, bewailing the degeneracy of the waters and the scarcity and shyness of the fish. Because they had always previously had luck early in May, they could not understand why they should now fish in vain, fished they ever so expertly. I, of course, did my best to comfort them, and assured them of good sport if they had the patience to wait for it, but that they might as well expect to find full-blown lilies upon the surface of a frozen lake as brook-trout in the rising mood while the streams were roiled by the fast-flowing snow-water.

A few sunny days after the 25th accomplished what was needful. Fish may be caught in the lakes, by trolling, as soon as the ice disappears, but even lake-trout are lazy, or "hug the bottom," until they are quickened into life or lured to the surface by sunshine and warm weather. As I am writing, I notice a very pleasant letter in the Journal of Commerce, from a venerable angler, in which he plaintively refers to his ill-luck early in May. And his experience was the experience of every one. It was, this year, the 25th before there was good fishing. All who came in earlier were disappointed; and those who took their departure before the 30th, doubtless did so with the false impression that here as elswhere, trout fishing was "played out." If so, they were simply mistaken. The present generation of anglers will be "played out" long before trout fishing in the Adirondacks. To be sure, the scamps who placed pickerel in Long Lake, and the Fish Commissioners who planted black bass in the Raquette did what they could to accomplish this result; but there will be trout in those waters long after those who perpetrated this folly shall have passed over their rods and reels to their successors.

The high water caused by the dam at Setting-Pole rapids is working great mischief in all this region. It has caused the overflow of tens of thousands of acres. The result will be that the beauty of the Raquette and its connected lakes will be marred by the destruction of the beautiful evergreens and maples which line their banks, and which have rendered them so wonderfully attractive and picturesque. But this is not all. The receding waters in midsummer must leave this whole region a reeking mass of decaying vegetation, filling the air with fever-exciting miasma, and making a sojourn in the midst of it exceedingly hazardous. Its effects are already seen in the thousands of dead trees which mar the beauty of the river's banks, and the coming August will demonstrate its pernicious influence upon the comfort and health of visitors, and the scattered residents upon its borders. If the effects apprehended are realized, the dam will be abated as a nuisance, by lawful process or otherwise — unless indeed the threatened suits for damages by parties aggrieved shall induce its owners to rid themselves of troublesome litigation by destroying the dam themselves.

Anglers are chiefly aggrieved by this obstruction to the free flow of the water because it has destroyed several favorite trout-haunts — notably Cole's Point and Lothrop's Chopping, where for many years I have had my best spring fly fishing. The eight or ten feet artificially added to the body of the water have so changed the currents of the river that they are no longer gathering places for trout. But in spite of this desecration, these old waters still afford ample amusement for those who fish them patiently and with moderate skill.

CHAPTER XXVII.

FOREST WANDERINGS — ECCENTRICITIES OF MEMORY — A LONG CONTEST.

Look you ! here is a trout will fill six reasonable bellies.—
[*Sir Izaak Walton.*

THE lower Saranac is closely fished, but it still affords good sport with the troll. The lake-trout are generally of medium size, varying from two to eight pounds, and occasionally running as high as ten and twelve. There are not many lakes in the woods so persistently fished, and not many which make better returns to the patient angler. There are a few gentlemen who seldom go beyond it and its connected waters, notably the venerable Mr. ARNOLD, of Keeseville, whose nearly fourscore years are kept mellow by the time he gives to this healthful recreation. Others, who have reached the sear-and-yellow-leaf time of life, would find their setting sun reflecting back a cheerier light if they would imitate his good example.

In August there is not much better fly fishing in all these woods than can be had in Cold and Ray brooks, which empty into the Saranac within a few miles of Martin's; and the trout are large as well as abundant. But only a few stop to fish there, hoping, often mistakenly, that a longer journey will insure them better sport. But many "go farther and fare worse." In the spring, however, to "go farther" is a necessity, as these brooks are not worth visiting before midsummer.

I have very pleasant recollections of my two visits to them, last year and the year before, far on in the month of August. Lying some three or four miles off from the straight line to the Raquette, I had not, until two years ago, deemed it worth while to experiment in new waters during the brief time I take in August, and so had always previously pushed on to my old haunts, but not always to my entire satisfaction.

The spring is the time for exploration, and I find no greater pleasure than in following my pilot over untrodden paths, with no other guide than is afforded by the pocket compass or the blazed tree. The tramp is sometimes wearisome, but always charming, both in anticipation and in realization. As I look back upon these excursions, a thousand delightful reminiscences come to me as freshly and as vividly as if some of them did not reach back more than a score of years — long before my locks were frosted or my vision dimmed; recollections of shady nooks, where rays of sunlight came down through the rustling leaves like lines of silver; of huge masses of gray rock, imbedded in thick moss, softer and more inviting than the luxurious divans of the drawing-room; of the "expressive silence" of the old woods, when, after the ascent of some rugged hill, we sat down to rest, indifferent, amid such surroundings, to the admonitions of prudence or the march of time. Enveloped in a golden sunset, with the forest birds making the woods vocal with their sweet melody, and with my own heart in unison with all these harmonies of nature, I have often found myself, with no other feelings than those of devout reverence and gratitude, repeating the words of the Psalmist: "How excellent is thy loving kindness, O God! therefore the children of men put their trust under the shadow of thy wing."

It is, as I have said, in the spring time that I make these diversions from the beaten path, and I have more than once thus discovered unfished waters, where, since "the morning stars sang together," no line had been cast or trout captured. They remain as sunny places upon the map of my memory, and are often revisited, although now upon the borders of some of them may be seen the hunter's camp and the fisherman's shanty.

And talking of memory, what a wonderful faculty it is! How drolly things long forgotten sometimes come back to us, without effort and without thought, like a vision, as if the events of ten or twenty years agone had occurred but yesterday! The books are full of curious instances. I have a few not in the books, but apropos to my theme, and which, while I am moving slowly on my way to the Raquette, may afford some one a moment's amusement.

One morning, twenty years ago, while encamped on the Fourth lake of the Fulton range, I was sitting on a freshly fallen spruce tree adjusting my reel for work, when the ever-welcome and long waited for call to breakfast was sounded. I hurriedly laid aside the reel and responded to the call. On sitting down to the table I found a disagreeable quantity of the exudations of the spruce tree adhering to my fingers. It troubled me to remove it, and what with that and the pleasures of the table, I was totally unable, afterward, to remember where I had left my reel, and was obliged to provide another for my day's fishing. Two years afterward I chanced to camp on the same spot, and while idly moving about I discovered a hacked spruce tree from which had exuded large globules of gum, clear as crystal. In breaking it off, some particles unpleasantly adhered to my fingers, when, like a flash, all the incidents of the old time came to my mind, and without a moment's hesitation I walked to the old spruce tree where I had then been adjusting my reel, and picked it up on the very spot where it had fallen two years before.

Here is another instance: More than fifty years ago, when a very little fellow, in company with others, I was lost in the woods. After many miles of weary wandering we came out upon a clearing, half famished. But the only food we could procure with which to appease our hunger was boiled potatoes and salt pickles. They must have been delicious, for to this day I never see a potato and pickle in juxtaposition without being carried back these fifty years, and see directly before me the earth-covered potato-heap from which the "boiling" was taken, the begrimmed pork barrel out of whose ponderous depths the pickles were abstracted, and the huge "crane" which swung across the huger chimney within whose ample "jams" the potato-pot was boiled. I have had a penchant for potatoes and pickles ever since.

Still another: One who, before disease had laid its heavy hand upon him, was wont to accompany me upon all my angling excursions, had the misfortune to become the possessor of a counterfeit five-dollar bill. As, poor fellow, his heart was always fuller of kind thoughts and generous purposes than his pocket-book of bank bills, he very naturally racked his brain to remember from whom he had obtained the rascally counterfeit. Months afterward it was still in his wallet, and he was in the habit of showing it to his friends to test their skill as judges of genuine currency. On one occasion, more than a year after he became the possessor of the bill, an expert pointed out to him a tiny spot upon it, which, to the expert, furnished incontestible proof of its character. In bringing the bill close to his eyes to discover the defect to which his friend had directed his attention, he held it near his nostrils and instantly detected *the odor of fresh beef*. After a second sniff, he stepped back with an air and attitude as tragic and as artistic as ever Forrest assumed in his role of Metamora, and exclaimed:

"I now do know the sanguinary wretch
Who thus hath tricked me of my honest gains;
And by the rood [he meant rod] which gentle Izaak plied,
I'll make the fiend disgor-r-r-ge.

This bill came to me from my butcher!"

And such was the fact. The delinquent remembered having missed a counterfeit five which he had kept hidden, as he supposed, but which, by some accident, had found its way into the till which contained genuine money. My friend has thought well of his nose ever since.

But who has not passed through a like experience, where the odor of a flower, the swing of the arm, a single note of long forgotten music, the curve of a fence, a flash of lightning, the whistle of the winter's wind, a smile, a sigh, a laugh, a word, a tone has brought back scenes, friends, incidents and situations which, but for these fleeting reminders, would have remained buried in the memory until the coming of that more mysterious transition when "all we ever did or said or felt shall, like a marshaled host, pass in full review before the immortal mind."

And now having, during this little bit of irrelevancy, passed over the five miles which intervene between Martin's and the river entrance to Cold and Ray brooks, where I went the last two Augusts, I wish only to say that, in the proper season, they will afford, with moderate skill and patience, such sport as is rarely vouchsafed to any angler anywhere. At least, such was my experience two years ago, when during a short afternoon I landed from a deep pool in Cold brook fifty splendid trout, *and fished three hours for one.* It was on this wise: For an hour or more before sunset, a trout which I estimated to weigh more than three pounds kept the water in constant agitation and myself in a fever of excitement. I cast for him a hundred times at least. With almost every cast he would rise, but would not strike. He would come up with a rush, leap his full length out of the water, shake his broad tail at me as if in derision, and retire to repeat his aggravating exploits as often as the fly struck the water. Other trout rose, almost his equal in dimensions, and were taken, but their capture soon ceased to afford me the slightest pleasure. The sun was rapidly declining. We had eight miles to row, and prudence dictated a speedy departure. But I was bound to land that trout "if it took all summer." I tried almost every fly in my book in vain; I simply witnessed the same provoking gyrations at every cast. If, however, I threw him a grasshopper disconnected from my line, he would take it with a gulp; but the moment I affixed one to the hook and cast it ever so gently, up he came and down he went unhooked, with the grasshopper intact. I was puzzled, and as a last resort I sat quietly down hopeless of achieving success so long as light enough remained for the wary fellow to detect the shadow of rod or line. The sun soon set. Twilight gently began its work of obscuration, and in due time just the shadow I desired fell upon the surface of the pool. I then disrobed my leader of its quartette of flies, put on a large miller, and with as much caution as if commissioned to surprise a rebel camp, and with like trepidation, I chose my position. Then, with a twist of the wrist which experts will comprehend, I dropped my fly as gently as a zephyr just where the monster had made his last tantalizing leap, when, with the ferocity of a mad bull and with a quick dash which fairly startled me in the dim twilight, he rose to my miller, and with another twist of the wrist, as quick and as sudden as his rise, *I struck him!* I have been present in crowds when grand victories have been suddenly announced, and when my blood has rushed like electric currents through my veins as I joined in the spontaneous shout of the multitude, but I have passed through no moment of more intense exhilaration than when I knew, by the graceful curve of my rod and by the steady tension of my trusty line, that I was master of the situation. He pulled like a Canastoga stallion, and "gave me all I knew" to hold him within the restricted circle of the deep pool, whose edges were lined with roots and stumps and things equivalent. It was an half hour's stirring contest, and the hooting of the owl in the midst of the darkness which enveloped us was the trout's requiem. When I had landed him and had him fairly in quad, will it be deemed silly for me to say that I made the old woods ring with such a shout as one can only give when conscious of having achieved a great victory?

CHAPTER XXVIII.

SILENT MEN — A LONG LOOK AHEAD — COCKNEY FISHERMEN — TROUT HABITS.

Think not silence the wisdom of fools, but, if rightly timed, the honor of wise men who have not the infirmity but the virtue of taciturnity, and speak not of the abundance, but of the well-weighed thoughts of their hearts. Such silence may be eloquence and speak thy worth above the power of words. Make such a one thy friend, in whom princes may be happy and great counsels successful. Let him have the key of thy heart who hath the lock of his own, which no temptation can open; where thy secrets may lastingly lie, like the lamp of Olybius his urn, alive and light, but close and invisible.—[*Sir T. Browne.*

At Trout-Hall, not far from this place, where I propose to lodge to-night, there is usually an angler that proves good company. And let me tell you that good company and good discourse are the very sinews of virtue.—[*Sir Izaak Walton.*

IN my frequent journeyings through these pleasant lakes and rivers, with no other companion than my guide, I have learned to understand how really loquacious are silent men of meditative mood. For hours together they make no sign; and but for an occasional smile, which passes like a ripple of sunshine across their composed and peaceful features, they might be deemed as unconscious and as unsusceptible as the iron row-locks whose monotonous music makes regular record of the march of time. But their silence is only in seeming. They are all the while holding sprightly mental conversation with absent friends, with favorite authors, with the mountains and forests and lakes which surround them, or are rehearsing some pleasant incident of field or flood to some sympathizing acquaintance, who is as really present, giving attentive audience, as if separated from them by but an arm's length instead of a hundred miles. I have seen such thoughtful wise men startled from their revery, who seemed surprised that they were not surrounded by a bevy of companions. This power of abstraction is a rare and pleasant gift. It differs in itself and in its possessors from absent-mindedness, which with me is always associated with glum moroseness, or at least with an absence of joyous geniality. But the jolliest-hearted may, under favoring circumstances, be abstracted, and wake up from his revery without losing a single ray of the pleasant sunshine with which his happy countenance is always illumined. It is not so with the chronically absent-minded, who may be heavy-browed but vinegar-visaged and constitutionally morbid, and who would no sooner think of angling than of robbing the exchequer of the realm.

An editor's life is neither the best nor the worst in which to cultivate this rare gift. There are those in the profession who can so concentrate their thoughts that even the pertinacious pleadings of a score of office-seekers cannot tangle the thread of their meditations; and sometimes even the least gifted among us have to throw off sentences amid such persistent din that Bedlam itself would seem the abode of silence. What little of the art came to me by nature and compulsory practice has been strengthened by the opportunities for silent meditation afforded by the habit of angling. My guide, who knew and humored my moods, was not, therefore, greatly startled when, in passing the approach to Cold brook, I broke the long silence with the very unintelligible exclamation: "He was a cunning old rat." It was the climax of a half hour's cogitation upon the protracted waiting and watching which finally resulted in the capture of the three-pound trout in the form and manner recounted in my last chapter. My guide very quietly responded (as if instinctively divining the subject of my meditations) to my involuntary observation with the simple question: "Did you land him?" And then I became as voluble as I had before been silent in recounting to him the incident already related to my readers. And just this is the thread upon which I have strung this bit of "abstraction."

At the rapids, about midway between the lower and middle Saranac lakes, there is as pretty a place from which to cast as can be found in the world. You stand upon solid rock, slightly elevated above the rapid-flowing stream, and can throw, if you have the skill, without fear of bush or brake, an hundred feet. It is the first opportunity one has, *en route*, after his long winter's rest, to shake out the wrinkles of disuse. I sometimes wonder whether, on some pleasant day in May, not long hence, I shall stand on this sunny spot, where I have stood during some portion of every season these twenty years, and find, in attempting to make my usual cast, that my "right hand has forgot its cunning." As old age cools the blood and dims the vision, and checks the elasticity of brain and limb, such thoughts sometimes come to the most buoyant, and often cast a shadow across the sunniest landscape. But it is only a shadow. With the thought comes up the vision of another river, brighter and clearer and purer than that which flows with such gentle gracefulness at my feet — "a pure river of water of life, clear as crystal, proceeding out of the throne of God and of the Lamb." It is a vision which reconciles all thoughtful anglers to the quick-coming time when these pleasant places, which now know them, shall know them no more forever.

For the first time in all my experience, I had no response here to my persistent appeals for a rise. There were a hundred spots within easy cast, which looked inviting. By some undefinable association, I found myself parodying that pleasant old song, "A Cot in the wood"— probably because of the applicability of two of its lines to my present surroundings:

> "And I said, 'If there's trout to be found in the world.
> The hand of an expert may hope for them here.'"

But if they were "here," they failed to respond. I tried eddy and current, rapid and pool, deep water and shallow, all to no purpose. With a "Well, this *is* strange," I reeled up, took my accustomed seat and moved off as disconsolate as a disappointed seeker of office. It was some consolation to learn, as I did soon afterward, that two or three novices had been "sloshing 'round" the rapids and still water, with bait and troll, for several hours before our arrival, and had just left as we landed. They may have caught some fish, but it is a marvel to me often how some of the visitors to these waters ever "get a bite." They use rods large enough for a shark, lines like miniature bed-cords, hooks seemingly made for the nose of the leviathan, with sinkers which fall into the water with a splash which would frighten any sensible trout "out of his propriety." But, somehow such fellows do lure fish to their ponderous bait; and that they do so is the strongest evidence that could possibly be given of the abundance of trout still remaining in these waters.

But lest, from what I have said of my want of success at this favorite spot on this occasion, some who remember it as pleasantly as I do myself, may heave a sigh of regret at its degeneracy, I had better say right here, although a little out of consecutive order, that on my return three weeks afterward, I found it to be "all my fancy painted it," and all my long previous experience had found it to be. It was getting well on in the afternoon, we had ten miles to row, and I was as nearly satiated with angling as I ever expect to be, but I could not forego the opportunity to make a cast or two as we dashed through the rapids homeward. The first throw brought a fine fish to the surface. I struck him as gently as the law of angling permits, and duly landed him. Another and another and another, in rapid succession, came at my call with a promptness and a rush which renders this last half hour of my three weeks' fishing a very pleasant memory. A dozen, gorgeous in their beauty, lay at my feet with a dozen more "making the water boil" in their eagerness to "get in out of the wet;" but I had no use for them, and with a merry nod to the trout and a long look at the old rock we left behind us, we reeled up and went on our way rejoicing.

There are several points between these rapids and Bartlett's, five miles distant, where any one unused to these waters, and the habits of trout, would expect success at any season — deep spring holes and cold brook outlets. But it is only a waste of time to fish them before the first or middle of July. Trout have their summer watering places as well as tourists; and it is not until the heated denizens of the towns and cities begin to move off toward Newport and Saratoga that these aristocratic tenants of our inland brooks and rivers leave the rapids and "riffs" for the cooler retreats of deep pools and refreshing spring holes.

This is one of the first lessons I learned in the art of angling. I had ridden fifty miles over a rough road on a hot day in August, to a stream where, according to the universal verdict, trout were as "plenty as blackberries." I placed myself under the guidance of a gentleman whom I supposed "knew the ropes" and upon whom it would be safe to lean. Early on the morning after reaching our destination, following his lead, I plunged into the stream — translucent as the atmosphere — and began to whip right and left, for a rise. Occasionally we would be rewarded by the capture of an ounce trout, who had evidently "lost its mammy," and so got lost itself; but after wading some two miles, we had not caught fish enough to cover the bottom of our creels. My friend was nonplussed, and so was I; but while far in the rear and quite ready to vote fishing a bore, I accidentally cast my fly into a cozy looking cove, when, on the instant, a pound trout rose and was captured. The experiment was repeated and re-repeated with the same result, when I called to my mentor, announced my luck, and suggested a change of tactics during the rest of the day. I had struck a spring hole, and in twenty minutes had caught more fish than both of us had taken during the three hours we had been whipping the shallows and "riffs" in the center of the stream. We afterward only fished in spring holes and at the mouths of spring brooks, and had no further reason to question the veracity of the friends who had lured us thither.

It is this habit of the trout which often brings disappointment to the novice. He fancies that because a stream is a trout-stream that trout should be found at all seasons in all parts of it. But I would as soon think of looking for a friend in an ice-house in January as for a trout in a cold spring hole in May or early in June. They are then in swift and shallow water, if such water is accessible, and there is where the expert looks for and finds them. It would be just as useless to look for trout in his spring haunts in August as to look for him in his summer haunts in May. Intermediately, from the middle of June to the middle of July, they are on the move. It is their transition period, when they are everywhere in small numbers, but abundant nowhere. And during this period there are probably more visitors in the woods than during any other thirty days of the year. If they have any hankering for fish or any taste for angling, they could not select, through the whole season, any period less propitious. Hence it is no uncommon thing for parties in the woods at this time to find it absolutely impossible to catch fish enough for use. But this is not surprising. Experts are too wise to go fishing during these thirty days, and only experts could lure any considerable number of fish, by any process, while they are thus passing from the swift waters to the quiet spring holes.

It was my fortune upon one occasion, when homeward bound, far on in June, to fall in with a party of six or eight who were camped where a fortnight before the trout were so abundant that I could catch a day's supply for a dozen men in a couple of hours. But I found this party literally fishless, and the most profoundly disgusted group of disconsolates I ever saw. Some of them had been there before, in proper season, and had done splendidly; and they had brought their friends with them now, anticipating equal success. I explained to them their mistake, recounted to them my own experience of a fortnight before, and, out of sheer sympathy, escorted them two miles to a favorite and secluded pond, where the trout are equally plenty at all seasons, and where they were made happy by abundant sport. Not one of these gentlemen ever afterward "fooled away his time" by fishing on the "riffs" when the trout had changed their quarters to the spring holes.

The somewhat monotonous outlet between the lower and middle Saranac opens into Round Lake, from the upper part of which, one of the grandest mountain views reveals itself to be had in all the woods. I have counted thirty well-defined peaks, the whole combined by a series of gracefully undulating curves which delight the eye of every appreciative lover of nature. My friend Palmer, the sculptor, carries this view in his memory today, and it will not be obliterated by any thing he may see in his present rambles among the grander, but no more beautiful mountain views of Switzerland.

Bartlett's somewhat famous hostelry stands at the head of this lake and is the summer resort of several greatly esteemed brethren of the angle — notably Dr. Romeyn, of Keeseville, whose twenty odd annual visits to these woods have only rendered them the dearer and the more attractive to him. He has caught the true spirit of the art, and is as cheery and joyous in camp as he is genial and accomplished in social life. And so is William A. Wheeler, who seeks and finds here the repose and invigoration which enables him to discharge his official duties at Washington with such exemplary promptness and fidelity. I doubt whether the highest office in the gift of the people would tempt him for a moment, if its acceptance would deprive him of the pleasure and benefit he derives from his annual visit to these pleasant woods and waters.

A short walk takes us over "Indian Carry," and a short row across the lake to Corey's — where I always manage to dine or sup, because Mrs. Corey is the best cook in the woods, and never fails to give me a cup of coffee as I taught her to make it fifteen years ago. There is, besides, generally some quiet angler sojourning here, whose company and conversation always insures a pleasant evening. I know of no better place between Plattsburgh and Potsdam to rest.

CHAPTER XXIX.

AN OLD RESIDENT — FINE SPORT — A FLY THEORY EXPLODED.

Oh! the gallant fisher's life,
 It is the best of any;
'Tis full of pleasure, void of strife,
 And 't is beloved by many:
   Other joys
   Are but toys,
   Only this
   Lawful is;
   For our skill
   Breeds no ill,
But content and pleasure.
 [*Sir Izaak Walton.*

PASSING from Corey's across a half mile carry, we strike a series of ponds which empty through Stony brook into the Raquette. Many years ago, when I first came here, this carry was covered with a dense growth of beautiful pines. But the demand for lumber was too pressing to be resisted, and this still delightful spot is denuded of its most attractive feature. The work of lumbering is being pushed vigorously within practical distances of all the water-courses of sufficient volume to float the logs to manufacturing points, of which Plattsburg, Potsdam and Glen's Falls are the principal. During the winter the logs are cut and placed upon the ice, ready for the spring freshets, and from the time of breaking up until well on in May, there is scarcely an available stream which is not filled with these moving masses. And yet the Rev. Mr. Murray, in his famous book, contrasting the Adirondacks with the forests of Maine, says of the former that they retain their primitive beauty because "the sound of the woodman's ax has never been heard" among them. If the reverend gentleman's theology is as loose as his facts, it must be a poor commodity.

But these annual drafts upon this wilderness are scarcely perceptible to the casual observer. Pine and spruce and hemlock constitute but a very small percentage of the entire forest, which remains seemingly as dense as if the woodman's ax had really never been heard here or the lumberman had never responded to the demands of commerce.

Stony brook (through which we pass to the Raquette) besides the water of its two or three ponds, has the flow from Ampersand brook, which has its supply from Ampersand pond, which lies some five miles up the mountain. The outlet of this brook is famous for its summer fishing, but it has never been my fortune to strike it at just the right moment to find practical confirmation of the truth of the large stories which are told about it. But I can believe them, for its source and surroundings are exactly adapted to make it a great gathering place for trout during the hottest of the summer months.

In these Stony brook ponds we have our first illustration of the effect of the high dam which has recently been built at Setting Pole rapids. The water was full eight feet above its natural level — an advantage only in this, that it enabled us to make an almost "straight wake" for the Raquette, instead of following the indescribably tortuous channel of the brook.

Near the point where this brook strikes the Raquette there has resided, solitary and alone, for many years, a man well-known to the frequenters of these woods. His house is primitive but quite spacious, and is surrounded by forty or fifty acres of well cleared land, of more than average productiveness for this region. Although living thus remote from neighbors and civilization, he is of more than ordinary intelligence, of a philosophical and metaphysical turn of mind, keeps closely posted in regard to trade, commerce, politics and general science, is and has been for many years an attentive reader, is hospitable, courteous and eccentric. He is, withal, an ardent lover of music, and before time and hard work had robbed his digits of their pliability, nothing gave him greater pleasure than to entertain his guests by exhibitions of his skill upon his favorite instrument, the violin. He is the trusted agent of several large land-owners, has more ready cash (rumor says) than some of his employers, and does more good with it than many who make far greater parade of their wealth and benevolence. And yet he has neither watch nor clock in his domicile. When the question was put to him: "Mr. Calkins, without a timepiece of any kind in the house, how do you know when to get up?" "Oh," said he, "I always get up when it stops raining"— not a bad rule, certainly, for a gentleman whose business does not require him to imperil his health by exposing it to the weather. I think I discovered in my last visit that the old gentleman was less fond of his solitary life than formerly, and yearned anxiously for the society which he enjoyed in his youth and which is so essential to one's comfort in old age. When he does leave these woods, he will be missed, for he has been a pleasant companion to a great many anglers, who appreciated his character and peculiarities.

The row down the Raquette, with its overflowed banks and strong current, was extremely pleasant. There was this drawback, however, that the high water robbed the river, in its immediate surroundings, of much of its beauty. We missed many old landmarks, and because of the overflow, passed a great many points where, before this piece of artificial vandalism (the high dam meaning) had worked its work, we were wont to find our best fishing. But after-success made ample amends for our present disappointment. On the 27th of May it was our good fortune to strike "the rapids" (so called) near "Big Ox-bow," — famous as a trout haunt for a few days in the Spring, while the fish are passing up stream from the lower waters. We were apprehensive that the unparalleled high water had destroyed this favorite resort, as it had a hundred others. But our fears were unfounded. I never knew the trout so abundant or so full of life. In two hours we killed twenty fish, which weighed $31\frac{1}{2}$ lbs.— one of them three pounds and a half, plump. We could have quadrupled our catch during the afternoon had we been so disposed. But we could not use them, and we had no desire to imitate the bad example of too many anglers, who take fish as long as they will rise, even though they are obliged to leave them on the shore to rot. Many tons are thus destroyed every year by those who lack the "quality of mercy" which is inherent in the true angler. There should be a stringent law against such shameful waste. It is as deserving of the pillory as sheep-stealing. Others subsequently had great success at this same point; but

I have heard of no two hours' fishing which averaged so roundly.

Greatly pleased with our success at "the rapids," but desiring to push on to other pleasantly remembered resorts, we were soon at Tupper's Lake — one of the most beautiful and majestic lakes in the wilderness. But there was no temptation to remain long upon its immediate borders. The high water had so affected the currents that many of the places I had been used to fish were no longer gathering places for trout. Hence, instead of, as usual, passing two or three days at these old camping grounds, and at the "high rocks" and swift waters in the neighborhood, we passed them by with a single cast or two, to one of which a pickerel responded, a sigh and a smothered malediction (in the spirit of Uncle Toby), and pushed on past "Peter's Rocks" to "Setting Pole Rapids," where I have always had finer sport than at any other point in the wilderness. I was not at all sanguine now, because I did not know what effect the dam had had upon the depth and flow of the water below it. But at the first cast my doubts were dissipated. The response was prompt and vigorous, and for a week I enjoyed the luxury of an angler's paradise, of which more anon.

I first visited these rapids fifteen years ago. Some of them who were with me then have gone to their rest; among them my earliest and trusted guide, who knew more of woodcraft and of angling than any man I ever met. But George Morse now sleeps his last sleep in the Soldier's Cemetery at Washington, where his resting-place is marked by a simple head-stone, reared to his memory by his old friend, Gen. Spinner, who was "one of us" during this first visit, and whose genial humor and happy ways rendered that particular excursion, extending from Boonville to Potsdam, ever-memorable. The General seldom fished during the trip, except for minnows as bait for others. His delight was to gather ferns and leaves and mosses and shells and geological specimens with which to adorn his home cabinet. And this habit, with all his exhausting labors as treasurer of the United States, he has kept up from that day to this. Those who visit his private office in the treasury building at Washington will find its walls lined with beautiful clusters of these treasures of nature, all of his own gathering. They mark the simple tastes and habits of the man through whose hands hundreds of thousands of millions have passed during the last twelve years without a single dollar adhering unlawfully to his fingers. Would he be what he is in the responsible office he holds had he not first acquired the simple habits of an honest angler? His jealous care of his responsible trust now prevents him from visiting the North Woods; but he still "goes a-fishing." There are few points on the Potomac, within easy reach of Washington, where he has not angled. This, with his daily botanising, is his only recreation. He is an enthusiastic lover of nature, and, in his moments of leisure, takes great delight in discoursing of fish and fishing. When he goes to his long home, the people will lose an honest and diligent servant, and the fraternity of anglers an appreciative and genial companion.

It was during this first visit to these rapids that the pretty conceit was dissipated that the angler who had the greatest variety of flies stood the best chance of success. It had been my pride to exhibit my fly-book to wondering admirers, and to pass glowing eulogies upon the artistic skill of McBride, of Caledonia, whose deft manipulation of silk and feather made him in those days famous wherever delicate angling was a recognized accomplishment. There was no fly which his observation had ever suggested or his imagination ever conceived, of which I had not samples. Many of them were the most perfect imitations possible of the prolific productions of nature, but others, in their gorgeous beauty, might have been worshipped without trenching upon the limits of idolatry. Yet they were all labeled taking flies in their season! When I had faith in the idea that all luck depended upon the use of exactly the right fly for the time and the occasion — for early morning and for the close of day, for sunshine and shade, for fair weather and foul, for still water and rapids, for shallow water and pools, for river and brook, and for this and for that interminably,— I was kept pleasantly busy two-thirds of my time hunting for the right fly to take trout where no trout lay to be taken.

On first reaching these rapids many years ago, it chanced that I had lost my leader by carelessly using my fly-line as a troll through the still water. A large fish had taken one of the flies when I expected no such visitor, and by a careless movement of my rod, fish, leader and fly incontinently retired in indissoluble union, to come back to me no more forever. My tackling was in a boat far in the rear, and I had no patience, with the inviting rapids and promising eddies before me, to await its coming. I had "in my mind's eye, Horatio," just the dazzling ibis I wished to use. I was sure that that and nothing else would bring abundant grist to my mill. But I had no ibis, and was about to give up in sullen silence, and await the arrival of the tardy rear guard for what I deemed to be indispensable to success, when my guide suggested a combination of red and blue flannel as a substitute.

He had the red and I had the blue. An ordinary fish-hook, a penknife and a few twists of silk did the business. The extemporized fly was made up, adjusted, cast and taken as quickly as I have told the story, and far more successfully. The red and blue flannel lure, and the half score of trout I took with it, dissipated all my fine fancies about gorgeous flies, and ultimately reduced my fly-book to a half dozen varieties suitable for spring or summer, shady or sunny days and shallow or deep water. But even these are practically reduced to two or three, notably the brown and black hackle, the red ibis, the miller for evening, and, for very swift, deep water, a large purple and red nondescript. And yet I would advise all experts to keep a well-filled fly-book. It is a pleasure to experiment, and the educated eye takes delight in looking at the variety of colors, shapes and forms which the skilled workman in fly-art has provided as lures for the speckled beauties.

CHAPTER XXX.

FISHING AT SETTING POLE RAPIDS — TWO NOTEWORTHY INCIDENTS.

PISCATOR, Jr.— To come to this fine stream at the head of this great pool, you must venture over these slippery, cobbling stones. Believe me, sir, there you were nimble or else you were down! But now you are got over, look to yourself; for on my word, if a fish rise here, he is like to be such a one as will endanger your tackle. How now!

VIATOR — I think you have such command here over the fishes, that you can raise them by your hand as they say conjurors can do spirits and afterward make them do what you bid them; for here's a trout has taken my fly! I had rather have lost a crown. What luck's this! He was a lovely fish, and turned up a side like a salmon!—[*Charles Cotton.*

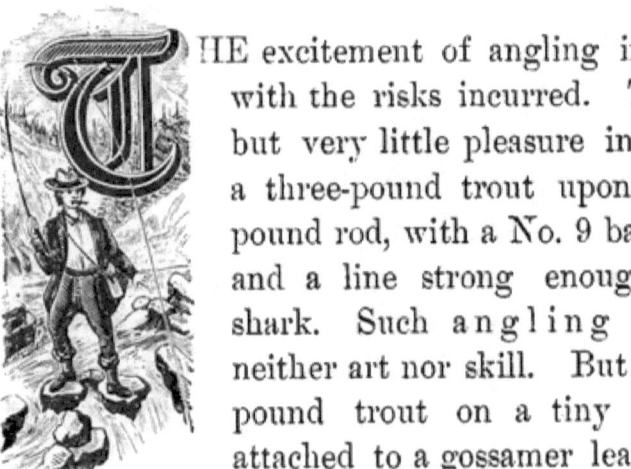

THE excitement of angling increases with the risks incurred. There is but very little pleasure in taking a three-pound trout upon a two-pound rod, with a No. 9 bait hook and a line strong enough for a shark. Such angling requires neither art nor skill. But a three-pound trout on a tiny fly-hook attached to a gossamer leader and line, the whole depending from an eight-ounce rod, and the trout struggling and leaping amid rapids dashing and foaming among jagged rocks — that is an experience which lifts the angler "into the seventh heaven," and gives him such exhilarating excitement that it remains to him a pleasant memory and "a joy forever." This is the sort of sport I always have at Setting Pole rapids, and never in larger or more perfect measure than during this present visit. Here are a few illustrations of the past and present:

A few years ago, before the dam was built, to reach the best points for casting it was necessary to stand upon some one of the numerous bowlders which lifted themselves above the water at the head of the rapids. When the water was well up, these standpoints were only reached over extemporized bridges composed of a single sapling extending from rock to rock, and often crossed at the hazard of a chilling plunge in the foaming rapids. I had reached the point I desired — a rock about the size and shape of a chair-bottom and slippery as ice from the wetted moss which covered its surface. On either side of it the water was six feet deep and very rapid. It was a hazardous stand from which to cast, but the most coveted within a circuit of thirty miles. After creeling a dozen very handsome fish, I resolved, with a feeling which anglers will appreciate, upon "just one cast more."

I made it, when the largest trout I ever saw in these waters rolled up to my fly, but I failed to strike him. I drew in and cast again, and again he rose, but the great resistance which his broad side presented to the swift current prevented him from overcoming the inch or two which intervened between his open jaws and my fly. But the dash was so eager that he threw himself entirely out of water, and I shouted to my guide, who was standing on the shore with distended eye and open mouth, "four pounds, if an ounce!" as my brown hackle again dropped just where I saw his broad fan-tail disappear at his last rise. Up he came with a rush; and before he lost his ascending momentum, I struck him with a thud! which gave me assurance that I had him securely hooked. For a moment he seemed content with the situation, but so soon as he discovered that he was not his own master, the tussle began. I struck him at thirty feet, in deep and swift but unobstructed water. I soon found that I could not hold him just at the point I desired, and was obliged to give him line. All went on finely for ten minutes. My eight-ounce rod nearly doubled upon itself, but stood the test charmingly; when, with a side rush which I could not prevent, he secured to himself the whole force of the current, and was distant a hundred feet in an instant. Within ten feet of the point he had thus reached was a cluster of rocks and a fall from which I must keep him or lose him. To hold him was like holding an unruly colt with a halter, and I soon discovered that he could not be started an inch homeward without "smashing things" in the attempt. As a last resort I called to my guide to wade in and net him. He responded at once, although the water reached his arm-pits, and the current threatened to take him from his feet at every step. To place the monster in the most favorable position possible, I gently forced him to near the side of a rock, that he might be the more easily reached. My guide made an honest effort, but in his excitement he struck wild, the fish was frightened and gave a spring which tore off the leader and let my released rod spring home with a bound which came near making me throw a back somersault into the foaming rapids, when I retired from the contest more heated in temper and blood than I had been before in a twelvemonth. But I soon became reconciled to the situation by arguing that such an half hour's contest was worth more than a thousand trout.

The next day, from the same spot, having four flies on my leader, I hooked four trout, aggregating five pounds in weight. In this swift water I had my hands full. But in due time they were subdued. The most difficult task was to land them from my contracted and slippery pedestal. I succeeded, however, by stooping down carefully and securing, by hand, each fish alternately as he lay in the water, except one, who broke the snell by chafing against the rock.

On reaching the rapids this year, I was not at all sanguine of success, even below the dam, whose construction had made such sad havoc with the best fishing points above. But I was soon relieved of my apprehensions. I had a prompt response to my first cast, and speedily landed a two-pound trout, the precursor of many more of the same sort, killed during our week's sojourn. And it was a week of supreme satisfaction. The rapids were full of trout, large, active and eager; and as there was a lumber shanty in the neighborhood, whose occupants were quite willing to receive all we sent them, we could satisfactorily dispose of the surplus portion of our catch. But very soon the supply was in excess of this demand, and I compromised with my conscience by throwing back all under two pounds. I dare not say how many were thus "rehabilitated," but enough, certainly, to furnish a rich harvest for my next year's visit.

Although I have had no such success in twenty years at this or any other point in all this region, I have only one thing which anglers would deem at all noteworthy to record. I was casting with my light fly rod in the swiftest water, when I had a strike which indicated unusual muscle. My click-reel flew round like a mill-spindle. I answered the call for "more line" until a hundred feet interposed between my slender tip and the fish, when I "cried a halt," as it was absolutely necessary to prevent him from passing over a rock which showed its foam-covered crest in his immediate neighborhood. This I found a difficult thing to do in such furious rapids, with the delicate rod from which the line depended. The heavy strain upon it had given it the curve of a perfect semicircle, and I was apprehensive that the addition of a single ounce would prove more than it could bear; but to reel up was a necessity. If the fish reached the impetuous current which passed on either side of the bowlder, something would break in the effort to check him. It was at this moment, when the contest was at its height, that *two* large trout revealed themselves as my prisoners. This revelation added to the interest of the contest, and seemed to render victory on my side entirely hopeless. But after twenty minutes of such intense excitement as only anglers will comprehend, I landed them both, without the aid of net or gaff; and they weighed together four pounds and a quarter, one weighing two pounds, and the other two pounds and four ounces. It would have been easier to have landed a single six-pounder. The play of such a strike is the acme of angling, and would be received by any expert as full compensation for a week's journey.

As an instructive lesson to fly-fishers, I may add that the tip which, with the care necessary in such a contest, bore this test of the excellence of its fibre, by being carelessly handled the next day, snapped under the pressure of a half-pound trout. The very best rod-makers are often anathematized for the inferior character of their material and their imperfect workmanship, when the anathema belongs to the stupid or careless angler. This tip had served me faithfully through two years of hard work, and it would have served me other years still, but for the folly of attempting to strike a mere minnow with the rod nearly perpendicular. When your rod exceeds an angle of forty-five, it is out of safe striking line. Better haul in for another cast than risk the break which will almost inevitably follow a heavy strike beyond that angle. I passed this pet tip into the depository of kindred wrecks, with the feeling which one experiences in bidding a long farewell to an old friend. I fear "I ne'er shall look upon its like again."

ADDENDA.

My respected associate, in a delightful letter from Watch-Hill, which was published the other day, concedes the attractive beauty of forest and river scenery, and the invigorating healthfulness of mountain air, but claims the palm for old ocean in both respects. A mutual friend, whose partialities lean forestward, sends us the following in reply:

TO "C. E. S."

I've read your letter—so you have a notion
That mount and lake must yield the palm to ocean?
Not so, my boy: I know you're orthodox,
And one small text your talk all endways knocks!
In that vast Heaven—which I hope you'll reach—
There rolls no ocean with its stretch of beach.
John, he of Patmos, in his splendid vision,
Saw no *salt* water 'mid the fields elysian—
That "*better* country," which is out of sight,
Has streams of crystal ever *fresh* and bright;
But John bears witness, and you must agree,
'Mid scenes all heavenly "*there'll be no more sea.*"

You write good letters 'way from brick and mortar,
But your sea-sentiment—will not hold water.

CHAPTER XXXI.

STALE FISH — IN A BAD FIX — REEL UP.

VENATOR.— When I would beget content, and increase confidence in the power and wisdom and providence of Almighty God, I will walk the meadows by some gliding stream, and there contemplate the lilies that take no care, and those very many other various little living creatures, who are not only created, but fed, man knows not how, by the goodness of the God of nature, and therefore trust in Him. This is my purpose; and so, " Let every thing that hath breath praise the Lord:" and let the blessing of St. Peter's Master be with mine.

PISCATOR.— And upon all that are lovers of virtue and dare trust in His providence, and be quiet, and go a-Angling. —[*Sir Izaak Walton.*

HOWEVER indifferent anglers may be in regard to the ordinary luxuries of the table, they have epicurean ideas about fish. A few hours makes a vast difference in the flavor of any fish; but with none is this fact more perceptible than with trout. Those anglers mean well who compliment their friends with a mess of fish a week old; but however carefully they may have been doctored and packed, they lose their delicate flavor and are stale; and a stale fish is an unpalatable morsel. While camping where a casting point was convenient (and it was rare when this was not the case), we never deemed it in good taste to cook a fish for breakfast which had been caught over night. If there are trout to be caught at all, you may be sure of a rise in the early morning; and you are equally sure of a delicious breakfast if you catch at five o'clock what you propose to eat at seven.

I have had a great deal of pleasant sport at Pearsfield Falls, the most picturesque bit of scenery in the woods. Those who have visited these Falls will remember the unique ledge which projects out upon their right side. I have caught trout from that point, at the very verge of the boiling cauldron, until my arms ached. But this year the water was too high to render that particular spot accessible, and I took to the boat to reach a favorite eddy, where usually trout gather. To do so required a long cast in the immediate proximity of a mass of saw-logs, which were swirling like fierce war-horses in the rapid current and surging eddies which held them fast prisoners in their whirling circle. The experiment, for a moment, looked like a success; but, in making a second cast for a good sized trout which, at the first effort, failed to reach the lure, a gust of wind swept my leader from its course, and instead of to the trout, which seemed eager to be taken, my fly hooked to a monster saw-log, which was pursuing its mad dance in the surging eddies. I "caved" at the possibility of landing so huge a catch, but was ambitious to save my tackling. The struggle was protracted and exciting, being in doubt whether, instead of saving my tackling, we would not ourselves be caught in the whirlpool, upon the very verge of which the struggle was progressing, and thereby give our friends at home an opportunity to laugh at our mishap or mourn at our funeral. But, fortunately, perhaps, in the adventurous spirit which had seized us, the saw-log was the victor. In making an unusual swirl, as it encountered some unusual eddy, helped by the bump of a score of others in a like predicament, my line snapped, and leader and flies were left prisoners of war, where they are still accompanying these fugitive saw-logs in their dizzy whirl at the foot of Pearsfield Falls. A few small trout, a sumptuous lunch, a drink of delicious water from one of the coldest springs in the wilderness, and several hours of unalloyed enjoyment, sufficed to fill our cup full of that quiet sort of pleasure which I find nowhere so abundantly as in these quiet forests.

My largest fish at Setting Pole rapids weighed three pounds. But I was enabled to go a pound better a few days afterwards at "Three-Pound Pond," a beautiful sheet of water, clear as crystal, in the neighborhood of the famous "Hitching's Pond"— which affords the best August fishing of any body of water in the woods. After a long siege of fly casting, with no other reward than a single fish of two pounds, I reluctantly resorted to the troll, when I was rewarded with a four pounder, the largest speckled trout I had ever captured. If I had taken him with a fly, I would have deemed it ample compensation for the time and expense of my trip. But that at least one "fish story" may be recorded truthfully, the trolling line and minnow are thus given the credit which belongs to them. I have often fished in this pond, and have taken therefrom many large trout, and it seems to hold no other, but I have succeeded, after patient trial, in taking but two with a fly. There may be points where, in July or August, the fly may be successful. But even this is doubtful, for the whole pond seems to be a bubbling spring, clear and cold, rendering it unnecessary for the fish to seek specially cool places in hot weather.

As usual, I took a run to Big Wolf Pond, where more large *lake* trout have been taken than in any other water inclosure in the woods, and where Dr. Perkins, two years ago, took his famous twenty-seven-pounder. But the glory of "Big Wolf" has departed. A ten-pound fish is the largest I have heard of being taken in its waters this year, and I trolled three hours without a strike. It has been trolled and speared and buoyed and set-lined to death. It will soon cease to be visited by any one.

But while I found the pond thus barren, the outlet was as fruitful of large brook-trout and black flies as ever. Amid such a swarm of the latter as would compel the instant retreat of any one not, as I was, thoroughly swabbed with tar oil, I caught several fish which weighed two and three pounds, the largest being the fattest and most beautifully marked fish I ever saw.

"Bog River Falls," at the head of "Big Tupper," proved so attractive that it held us in camp four days. The view from our camping ground, near the Falls, in sunshine or by moonlight, was entrancing. It revealed to us, at a glance, not only all the beauties of this most beautiful lake itself, but the cloud-capped summits of a score of mountains besides. "Grand," "beautiful," "majestic," "sublime," "transparent," "translucent," etc., etc., could all be used with propriety, were I in the descriptive mood. But, as this chapter is dedicated to fish and not to scenery, it is only proper to say that the large trout always found at the foot of the Falls, behaved handsomely, and graced our table daily with as delicate morsels as ever melted on human palate.

It is, however, neighborly to warn all anglers against the assumption that because they may find large and delicious fish at the foot of the Falls there must be equally large and delicate fish up the river. It took several years' experience to convince me that this idea was erroneous. The fish up the river are neither large, abundant nor of delicate flavor. And the farther up you go, the worse you are off, until you strike Hitching's pond. The fish found at the Falls find their feed and growth and flavor in Big Tupper and adjacent waters. There is something in Bog river which causes a deterioration; and it is worse still in Little Tupper and its outlet. There the fish are lean and of poor flavor — not in winter and early spring alone, for the trout of all waters are infested with unpalatable and unseemly parasites until they pass into the rapids in the spring — but at all seasons. This positive statement may "turn the stomachs" of some of my friends who like to visit this lake because its trout are sometimes large and always abundant. But I can't help it. Truth is truth, and unclean trout should not be eaten. Little Tupper is a great resort for deer, and it will pay sportsmen to go there for them. But I advise those who persist in complementing their roast venison with a dish of speckled trout to do, not as Mrs. GLASS suggests, "first catch and then cook," but first catch, then critically examine, and then eat " with what stomach you may."

After a week's further rambling, with delightful repetitions of pleasant days, charming scenery and abundant sport — at Hitching's pond, at Raquette Falls, Cold river, Big Rock, Split Rock and other places famous for the abundance and weight of their fish — we reluctantly turned our faces homeward. But not until we had had evidence of the rapidity with which pickerel are multiplying in these waters. As they rarely take a fly, I was disgusted but once with a rise from one of them. But those who trolled, particularly around the Falls and in the vicinity of Cold river, were constantly annoyed by them. And this annoyance will increase every year (for no fish multiplies more rapidly,) until trout fishing in the Raquette will cease to be the attractive amusement which it has been these thirty years, and which it still is to those who know how to fish.

I have all my life heard of the monster fish caught in the rivers of Maine, and although I have angled in almost all the waters from Quebec to Minnesota, I have yet to experience the pleasure of landing a seven-pound trout. This pleasure I hope to enjoy the coming season.* Meanwhile I bid adieu to the Adirondacks until another Spring-time shall return, when, if all is well, I shall again "go a-fishing."

---

* This hope was realized in June, '74, in Rangely lake. I was casting with my lightest rod, when a large fish struck my fly, and after a two hours' fight I landed a genuine brook trout, which weighed exactly seven pounds. I have a fine portrait of the fish, painted in oil on birch bark, by my friend Dr. OTIS, of New York, who was of the party. It is a beautiful picture, and I cherish it above rubies.

www.ingramcontent.com/pod-product-compliance
Lightning Source LLC
Chambersburg PA
CBHW032104220426
43664CB00008B/1131